Measure for Measure

Cedric Watts is Professor of English in the School of English and American Studies at the University of Sussex. He is the author of *Conrad's 'Heart of Darkness': A Critical and Contextual Discussion* (1977), *Cunninghame Graham: A Critical Biography* (with Laurence Davies, 1979), *A Preface to Conrad* (1982), *R. B. Cunninghame Graham* (1983), *The Deceptive Text* (1984) and *A Preface to Keats* (1985). He has edited *Joseph Conrad's Letters to R. B. Cunninghame Graham* (1969), *The English Novel* (1976), and *Selected Writings of Cunninghame Graham* (1981).

D1386946

Penguin Masterstudies

William Shakespeare

Measure for Measure

Cedric Watts

Advisory Editors: Stephen Coote
                              Bryan Loughrey

Penguin Books

Penguin Books Ltd, Harmondsworth, Middlesex, England
Viking Penguin Inc., 40 West 23rd Street, New York, New York 10010, U.S.A.
Penguin Books Australia Ltd, Ringwood, Victoria, Australia
Penguin Books Canada Limited, 2801 John Street, Markham, Ontario, Canada L3R 1B4
Penguin Books (N.Z.) Ltd, 182–190 Wairau Road, Auckland 10, New Zealand

First published 1986
Reprinted 1987

Made and printed in Great Britain by
Richard Clay Ltd, Bungay, Suffolk
Filmset in Monophoto Times

To Linda, William and Sarah

Contents

Part 1 Preliminary Matter

1.1 Editorial Notes and Acknowledgements

Quotations from *Measure for Measure* are from the Arden edition, edited by J. W. Lever (London: Methuen, 1965), apart from the Folio citations in section 3.1. Quotations from all other Shakespearian texts are from *The Complete Works* edited by Peter Alexander (the Tudor edition; London and Glasgow: Collins, 1951; reprint, 1966). Biblical quotations are from the Geneva Bible of 1560 (facsimile edition; Madison, Milwaukee and London: University of Wisconsin Press, 1969). In England in the late sixteenth and early seventeenth centuries this was the most popular and influential translation. Shakespeare used the Bishop's Bible (1568) in his early plays: but from about 1596, he generally used the Geneva Bible.[1]

In any quotation, a row of three dots (. . .) indicates an ellipsis already present in the printed text, whereas a row of five dots indicates an omission that I have made. In lines of verse, I have where necessary inserted a grave accent over any otherwise-unsounded syllable that needs to be sounded in order to preserve the metre. All other emendations to quoted passages are given in square brackets. With these exceptions, I have endeavoured to present all quoted material without correction or alteration.

Mr Alan Sinfield kindly helped to check the proofs.

1.2 Foreword

I first read *Measure for Measure* a long time ago: March 1955, in my last year at school. Reading Shakespeare's earlier comedies had sometimes been a chore; reading this one was a pleasure. Like many other school-pupils I had harboured a suspicion that Shakespeare might not be as good as he was always made out to be; at *Measure for Measure* the suspicion vanished, even if the Shakespeare who spoke from the page wasn't exactly the Shakespeare I'd been led to expect. The play offered realism, cynicism, bawdry, and a tough searching quality; it seemed odd, strange, jarring and aggressively intelligent, as though assailing conventional notions of comedy.

For example, there was the startling power of Claudio's outburst to his sister in Act III, scene i:

> *Ay, but to die, and go we know not where;*
> *To lie in cold obstruction, and to rot;*
> *This sensible warm motion to become*
> *A kneaded clod; and the delighted spirit*
> *To bath in fiery floods, or to reside*
> *In thrilling region of thick-ribbèd ice* . . . . .

What made it seem startling was not only the vivid intensity of the utterance but also the stark contrast that this speech made to the recent homiletic advice of the Friar-Duke. I was reading the play in a cheap one-volume *Complete Shakespeare* with small type, so that the two speeches, though separated by about a hundred lines, were there in front of me side by side, the Duke's on the left-hand page, Claudio's on the right. The Duke had eloquently and apparently authoritatively urged Claudio to a stoical acceptance of death:

> *Be absolute for death: either death or life*
> *Shall thereby be the sweeter. Reason thus with life:*
> *If I do lose thee, I do lose a thing*
> *That none but fools would keep. A breath thou art* . . . .

It had seemed authoritative, that long speech, as it unfolded. And now, within a page, was a starkly conflicting view of life and death, death as a location of fantastic horror and surrealistic torment, life as a paradise in comparison. The Duke had seemed wise and conscientious; he had spoken as a Friar, which surely gave hallowed authority to his homily. Yet Claudio was evidently the young hero of the plot, someone to regard sympathetically, and his eloquence had its own distinctive power, an impetuous force of image and tone. And there the two speeches were before me, side by side, saying totally opposed things. Who was right? One of them, neither, or in some elusive way both? What was certain was the deliberateness of the juxtaposition. Normal conventions of comedy seemed far less important in *Measure for Measure* than Shakespeare's determination to challenge ethical thought and feeling together; to search deeply into big problems; perhaps to let the structure of the play be determined more by the intelligence of embodied argument than by the exigencies of orthodox structure and expected entertainment.

Arguments about life and death, sex and marriage, justice and authority: repeatedly the play dramatized extremes of viewpoint, making matters vividly problematic – and also contemporary. It seemed to reach into the 1950s and beyond them; for its boldness and incisiveness mocked the inhibitions and respectabilities which prevailed in the provincial England of 1955. I inwardly cheered Pompey's 'Does your worship mean to geld and splay all the youth of the city?' and Lucio's 'A little more lenity to lechery would do no harm'; and, as a proleptic rebuke to the England in which capital punishment was still operative, the presentation of Barnardine seemed to be one of the glories of the text. You'll remember how Barnardine is introduced: the Duke has been outwitted by Angelo, who, instead of waiving Claudio's death-sentence, orders the execution to be hastened; and the Duke seeks someone to be killed in Claudio's stead. Barnardine seems to be designed by the plot as the surrogate victim. But when the Duke encounters Barnardine, he encounters a distinctively living individual, a stubbornly hung-over humanity; and the Duke can't go through with his plan: he can't, when he meets the man, actually muster the determination to say 'Off with his head!' And eventually the plot emits one Ragozine, a pirate who has conveniently died of fever just in time for his head to be used as a substitute for Claudio's. As part of the plot, then, Barnardine seems to be redundant; surely a dramatist aiming for narrative economy would have omitted him and proceeded directly to the news of Ragozine's death. Therefore the function of Barnardine seemed to be thematic and ethical: he was there to challenge the Duke, and thereby to challenge the very principle of capital punishment.

So *Measure for Measure* could seem, in the 1950s, not 'dark', 'morbid' and full of 'gloom and dejection', as it had been termed,[2] but healthily cogent. In the following decade grew the so-called 'permissive society' and its controversies; and they were the *Measure for Measure* controversies: about liberty versus licence, about spontaneity versus control, about anarchy versus order, about old religion and new scepticism. These arguments continue. George Bernard Shaw was right when he said that in this play we find Shakespeare 'ready and willing to start at the twentieth century if the seventeenth would only let him'.[3] *Measure for Measure* was long neglected and much disparaged. It has its oddities and its flaws. But nowadays, to students and theatregoers, to amateurs and specialists, its cogent eloquence is loud and clear.

1.3 The Plan of This Book

In Part 2, the emphasis is placed on the background and 'contexts' of *Measure for Measure*. There is a biographical section followed by sections which relate the play to other works of Shakespeare and which survey the main source-materials. In Part 3, I look in detail at the content of the play and consider various problems and critical approaches.

Naturally, the distinction between Parts 2 and 3 is merely one of emphasis and is not rigid. The play's sources may be part of its context, but their adaptation by Shakespeare is part of its content. A critical analysis may be predominantly concerned with the content, but inevitably it will incorporate assumptions about the historical and cultural background of the work. A monograph imposes a linear, consecutive sequence on matters which present themselves to the mind less as sequences than as mobile, interlinked and interchanging clusters. Rather than a scene-by-scene commentary on the play, I have chosen to offer a variety of approaches and perspectives. Although my prejudices will influence the whole, this format may give the reader a better opportunity to see and choose between the various options in interpretation; and such a relative openness may be in keeping with the spirit of *Measure for Measure* itself, which is so intensely concerned with the dramatization of feasible alternatives and contrasts.

Part 2   The Context of *Measure for Measure*

2.1   Shakespeare's Life and *Measure for Measure*

To begin with a familiar fact: William Shakespeare was baptized on 26 April 1564 at Stratford-upon-Avon, a small town in the rural west midlands of England, amidst richly productive agricultural land. What for Shakespeare was to be so consequential about an upbringing in this rural province is so obvious that we tend to take it for granted: his eventual works frequently express the sense of critical contrast between a countryside of fertile farmland, with its own rituals and customs, and the life of a city like London, with its teeming crowds, its bustle of trading, its taverns and brothels, its opportunities and its iniquities. Other great contemporaries of Shakespeare, notably Christopher Marlowe, Ben Jonson and Thomas Dekker, knew the city intimately; but in addition Shakespeare knew intimately the world of countryside, the birds, the hares, the deer, the harvest. Works as diverse as *2 Henry IV*, *As You Like It* and *The Winter's Tale* dramatize the sense that the city offers both civilization and decadence, both vitality and corruption, while the rural world, for all its rusticity and simplicity, may offer a different and saner rhythm, one linked to the seasonal cycle and age-old continuities. Even into the urban Vienna of *Measure for Measure* that cycle occasionally sends its imagery as a promise of a more wholesome order beyond the turbulence of the corrupted city: 'her plenteous womb / Expresseth his full tilth and husbandry'; 'Look, th'unfolding star calls up the shepherd.'

Shakespeare's mother was a landowner's daughter; his father, John, a farmer's son, was a glovemaker and trader in farm commodities. John Shakespeare was, for some time, evidently a prosperous and prominent townsman: after holding various public offices he became, in 1568, Stratford's Bailiff (equivalent to Mayor). Between 1576 and 1596 he sank from prominence, apparently because of business difficulties. He mortgaged his wife's property, was fined £20 for failing to appear in court to give security that he would keep the peace, was sued for part of his brother's debt, and avoided church 'for feare of process for debtte'. Then in the late 1590s he prospered again, perhaps helped by his son, and by 1601 he was once more a member of the borough council.

2.1 *Shakespeare's Life and* Measure for Measure

Of William Shakespeare's schooldays (as of much else in his biography) nothing is known for certain, but it is probable that he attended Stratford Grammar School, where the curriculum offered a thorough grounding in Latin rhetoric, logic and literature. Ben Jonson later alleged of Shakespeare, 'thou hadst small *Latine*, and less *Greeke*';[1] but what Shakespeare's works suggest is that though he had little Greek he had an immense amount of Latin – he was familiar not only with the great literary works (Seneca's plays and Ovid's *Metamorphoses*, for example) but also with innumerable Latin phrases, tags, maxims and *sententiae*, so that he virtually acquired a 'Latin subconscious mind'. Thus, the maxim 'Dormiunt aliquando leges, moriuntur nunquam' emerges in *Measure for Measure* (II.ii.91) as 'The law hath not been dead, though it hath slept'; and when, in the same scene, Isabella says:

> *Could great men thunder*
> *As Jove himself does, Jove would ne'er be quiet,*
> *For every pelting petty officer*
> *Would use his heaven for thunder* . . . . .
>
> (II.ii.111–14)

her words adapt Ovid's *Tristia*, II, 33–4:

> *si quoties peccant homines sua fulmina mittat*
> *Iuppiter, exiguo tempore inermis erat* . . . . .

These are just two of the numerous small examples that could be given. A more radical effect of Shakespeare's Latinism is found in the two great speeches on death in Act III, scene i. The speech of the Friar-Duke is strongly Stoical and is thought by commentators to draw on Seneca, Epicurus, Cicero, Apuleius and Palingenius. Claudio's more fervent speech contains elements deriving from Lucretius, Virgil (*Aeneid*, Book VI) and the anonymous *Somnium Scipionis*. In both cases, the effect is to make the speeches markedly less Christian in their eschatology than might have been expected. Whether death is seen as sleep (as the Friar-Duke suggests) or as nightmare (as Claudio imagines), the consolatory Christian idea of the loving God who promises eternal life seems to have been vanquished by the force of pagan imaginings.

Another of the sure facts of Shakespeare's life is that on 27 November 1582 a special licence was issued for the marriage of William Shakespeare to Anne Hathaway. He was then eighteen years old and she about twenty-six. The marriage presumably took place at the end of November; and six months later, on 26 May 1583, Anne's daughter Susanna was christened. One possible inference is that this had been a 'shotgun' marriage, the special licence having been hastily obtained when the couple learnt that Anne was pregnant by William. Another possibility, however, is that well before the church wedding ceremony, Anne and William were respectably married by a civil contract. Nobody knows. Whatever the truth, the reader will be reminded that in *Measure for Measure* the distinction between civil betrothal and holy wedlock is crucial to the plot, and it is interesting that the 'illegitimate' pregnancy of Juliet is seen in quite contrasting ways: as the dire consequence of lust and the shameful outcome of sin, yet also as the natural expression of love.

Shakespeare's daughter Susanna (1583–1649) lived to marry and have a daughter of her own. His son Hamnet (1585–96) died at the age of eleven, but Judith, Hamnet's twin sister, lived until 1662. While Shakespeare's wife remained in Stratford, he travelled to London and there established himself not only as a playwright and poet but also as an actor and eventually as a shareholder in the theatrical company. The famous denunciation by a rival author, Robert Greene, makes it clear that by 1592 Shakespeare was a disconcerting new force in the theatre:

there is an vpstart Crow, beautified with our feathers, that with his *Tygers hart wrapt in a Players hyde*, supposes he is as well able to bombast out a blanke verse as the best of you: and beeing an absolute *Iohannes fac totum*, is in his owne conceit the onely Shake-scene in a countrey.[2]

As an actor, Shakespeare is believed to have performed both serious and comic parts in plays by himself and others: he appears in the cast-lists of Ben Jonson's *Every Man in His Humour* and *Sejanus*. In 1594 he is named as one of the leaders of his company, the Chamberlain's Men (which in 1603 became the King's Men), and he remained with it until his retirement around 1611. In 1599 he is known to have become a shareholder in the Globe Theatre, with a one-tenth share, entitling him to an equivalent proportion of the profits; and evidently these were considerable, for during the subsequent fourteen years Shakespeare bought some property in London and substantial properties and areas of land at Stratford. New Place, which he bought for £60 in 1597, was the second largest house in the town, with two barns, gardens and two orchards. Hither he retired for the last years of his life, from approximately 1611 to his death in 1616.

What is obvious about Shakespeare's theatrical career is that he was not only a great critical success in his day, being recognized as pre-eminent in the drama by his contemporaries (as is shown by the various tributes which preface the First Folio), but also an immense commercial success with the theatregoing public. It cannot be emphasized too strongly that in the fiercely competitive world of Elizabethan and Jacobean drama,

with all its brilliant writers vying for popularity and success, the public –
not a coterie or a group of intellectuals or a courtly elite, but the general
public – gave their acclaim, above all, to Shakespeare.

Another point which is familiar but worth emphasizing is that the
richness of Shakespearian drama owes much to the social diversity of the
audience, which extended from the monarchy to the rogues and rabble of
the crowds. A law of 1572 obliged actors to secure the patronage of some
aristocrat or court official with a rank not below that of baron. The
patrons of Shakespeare's company were the Lords Chamberlain (the first
and second Lords Hunsdon) and, on the accession of James I, the King
himself. Shakespeare's plays were generally performed before the public
at the open-air theatre (e.g. the Globe) or, after 1608, at an indoor theatre
(Blackfriars); but in some cases they were also performed privately at the
house of some nobleman, or before the lawyers of the Inner Temple, or
(perhaps before the monarch) at court. *A Midsummer Night's Dream* was
evidently commissioned for a noble marriage; *The Tempest* was performed
before the king at Whitehall; and the first recorded performance of
Measure for Measure was also at Whitehall. If there were plague in
London, the company could tour the provinces. When Shakespeare was
writing his plays, he must frequently have borne in mind that the new
work might be performed before both a private and a public audience,
and in both an indoor and an outdoor setting. At the open-air theatre the
more affluent patrons would be seated in the covered boxes facing the
stage; and there is good evidence (in, for example, Jonson's *Every Man
Out of His Humour* and Dekker's *The Gull's Horn-Book*) that sometimes
such patrons were even seated upon the stage itself. The poorer patrons,
the 'groundlings', would stand on the ground before and at the sides
of the stage, which jutted out half-way across the auditorium. Dekker
wrote:

[T]he place is so free in entertainment, allowing a stool as well to the farmer's son
as to your Templar; that your stinkard has the selfsame liberty to be there in his
tobacco-fumes, which your sweet courtier hath: and that your carman and tinker
claim as strong a voice in their suffrage, and sit to give judgement on the play's life
and death, as well as the proudest Momus among the tribe of critic.....[3]

To this socially mixed audience (which contrasts so markedly with the
limited social range of the French audiences for the neoclassical drama of
the seventeenth century) we can readily relate the mixture of the learned,
sophisticated, bawdy, earthy, conservative and rebellious in Shakespeare's
texts. In *Love's Labour's Lost* and *A Midsummer Night's Dream* various
features, including the marked tone of courtly elegance, support the view

that these plays were first designed for a noble audience; but we should beware, however, of rapidly correlating one kind of material with one kind of imagined social class. The elegant ladies of *Love's Labour's Lost* are adept at dirty punning; and the bawdy Falstaff, who had been banished in *2 Henry IV*, reappeared as a lover in *The Merry Wives of Windsor* at the special request (tradition maintains) of Queen Elizabeth. Nor should we underestimate the intelligence of a popular audience which readily paid its pennies to see works as complex as *Hamlet* and *King Lear* – works in which Shakespeare exploits, questions and subverts conventional expectations. In the *Sonnets*, Shakespeare sometimes expresses a fastidious disdain for his profession:

> *Alas, 'tis true I have gone here and there*
> *And made myself a motley to the view .....*
> (sonnet 110)

> *And almost thence my nature is subdu'd*
> *To what it works in, like the dyer's hand .....*
> (sonnet 111)

Nevertheless, the 'mechanic slaves, with greasy aprons', and their like, were helping to raise Shakespeare to the status of a propertied gentleman of Stratford-upon-Avon; and when Hamlet speaks scornfully of 'the groundlings, who, for the most part, are capable of nothing but inexplicable dumb shows and noise', it is worth remembering that the original actor may well have been uttering those words within a few yards of a crowd of groundlings who were evidently able to appreciate that 'the purpose of playing ..... was and is to hold, as 'twere, the mirror up to nature'.[4]

In *Measure for Measure*, the action moves from the court to the streets, from a moated grange to a prison; the social range extends from the highest to the lowest; and the modes of discourse extend from ceremonial verse to vulgar prose. His socially mixed audiences gave Shakespeare incentives to range in ideas and techniques; but his society also imposed some constraints on what he might say. Various modes of censorship were available. A company which offended the authorities might lose its licence, its official warrant, and thus be forced to disband. New plays had to be submitted to the Master of the Revels, who acted as censor and licencer of plays for performance. Politically satiric and subversive matter was likely to incur his anger, and if such material did reach performance the author and even the actors might be jailed. Ben Jonson was imprisoned once for playing in, and being part-author of. the satiric *Isle of Dogs*. and once for his part-authorship of *Eastward Ho!* (which, at a time when a Scottish king was on the throne of England, had tactlessly mocked the Scots). Nevertheless, if the courts of Elizabeth and, subsequently, of James held powers of censorship, at least they actively encouraged the theatre as such; it was the middle-class Puritans, particularly militant among the tradesmen and City Corporation of London, who were the inveterate enemies of the players. They claimed that the plays set examples of immorality; that such conventions as the playing of women by boys encouraged perverse and lascivious thoughts; that on Sundays the theatres seduced the people from church attendance; and that the public playhouses were haunts of the dissolute and lecherous.[5] (When the Puritans came to power in 1642, one of their first moves was to close the theatres completely.) Not surprisingly, then, in the plays of Shakespeare and his contemporaries, it is the Puritans or Anabaptists or 'precisians' of various kinds who are repeatedly subject to satiric scorn or are revealed as ruthless hypocrites: the presentation of the 'precise' Angelo is a vigorous variation on a familiar theme.

When discussing censorship, the scholar F. E. Halliday remarks:

Shakespeare seems to have had little trouble with his plays, for they contain little satire and few topical allusions, while his political philosophy agreed well enough with that of Elizabeth, James I and Cecil. But the deposition scene in *Richard II* was not printed until Q4, 1608 . . . . .[6]

Whether his political philosophy 'agreed well enough' from conviction or prudence, or because the complexity of the works made them amenable to a variety of interpretations, is debatable: sonnet 66 deplores 'art made tongue-tied by authority'. Halliday's remark about *Richard II* is salutary. When reduced to concise paraphrase, Shakespeare's plays often seem to be broadly conservative. In *Henry VI*, *Richard II* and *Julius Caesar*, we see that the toppling of a legitimate ruler unleashes a wasteful turmoil of civil war; and in *Measure for Measure*, *King Lear* and *The Tempest*, those subordinates to whom a ruler delegates or relinquishes his power prove to be arrogantly ruthless. Yet if Shakespeare had believed that concise paraphrase was a sound guide to truth, he would not have become a dramatist; and in the fullness of his drama there are few political positions that are not questioned, and questioned incisively. If *Richard II* seems, with the hindsight provided by *1* and *2 Henry IV*, to be a 'conservative' text, we should not forget that some of Shakespeare's contemporaries saw it quite differently: on the eve of the Earl of Essex's unsuccessful rebellion in February 1601, some of his supporters paid Shakespeare's company forty shillings extra for a special performance of *Richard II* – including the deposition scene which had been omitted from the First Quarto text. Evidently they believed that it would help their cause if the people could be reminded that monarchs could be deposed and slain; and, later, Elizabeth is reported to have remarked angrily: 'I am Richard II, know ye not that? ..... This tragedy was played forty times in open streets and houses.'[7] What this suggests is, first, that Shakespeare could be seen as cogently topical even when dealing with apparently remote or distant events, and secondly that even in his lifetime the complexity of his works permitted their hearers or readers to see that they might serve a variety of outlooks.

As we shall see, there is evidence that *Measure for Measure* could be construed as flattery of King James I. It has also been construed as a parable in the spirit of the New Testament, and it has long been regarded as a peculiarly problematic work. Shakespeare's responsiveness to the diversity of social and cultural life in his day meant that in a text like *Measure for Measure* he was, among other things, performing a most important political task: he was extending the understanding of the political. Even the most private and intimate matters had their political dimension; but individual vitalities could persistently challenge ideological order.

In *The Elizabethan World Picture*, E. M. W. Tillyard argued that Shakespeare's imagination was thoroughly imbued with the great conservative orthodoxies which had so frequently been formulated between the Medieval and the Jacobean periods: particularly the conception of a cosmic hierarchy extending from the inanimate to God on high. Sir Thomas Elyot's *The Boke Named The Gouernour* (1531) gave a typical formulation:

Hath nat he [i.e. God] set degrees and astates in all his glorious warkes?
 Fyrst in his heuenly ministres, whom, as the churche affirmeth, he hath constituted to be in diuers degrees called hierarches ..... Beholde the foure elementes wherof the body of man is compacte, howe they be set in their places called spheris, higher or lower, accordynge to the soueraintie of theyr natures .....
 Beholde also the ordre that god hath put generally in al his creatures, begynnyng at the most inferiour or base, and assendynge upwarde: he made not only herbes to garnisshe the erthe, but also trees of a more eminent stature than herbes, and yet in the one and the other be degrees of qualitees; some pleasant to beholde, some delicate or good in taste, other holsome and medicinable, some commodious and necessary Semblably in byrdes, bestis, and fisshes, some be good for the sustinance of man, some beare thynges profitable to sondry uses, other be apte to occupation and labour; in diuerse is strength and fiersenes only; in many is both strength and commoditie; some other serue for pleasure; none of them hath all these qualities;

fewe haue the more part or many, specially beautie, strength, and profite. But where any is founde that hath many of the said propreties, he is more set by than all the other, and by their estimation the ordre of his place and degree euidentlye apperethe; so that euery kynde of trees, herbes, birdes, beastis, and fisshes, besyde theyr diuersitie of fourmes, haue (as who sayth) a peculier disposition appropered unto them by god theyr creatour: so that in euery thyng is ordre, and without ordre may be nothing stable or permanent; and it may nat be called ordre, excepte it do contayne in it degrees, high and base, accordynge to the merite, or estimation of the thyng that is ordred.[8]

'It is what everyone believed in Elizabeth's days,' comments Tillyard;[9] which invites the obvious rejoinder that if everyone believed it, the doctrine would not have been so insistently propagated by those in positions of authority. Such propaganda might rather imply a fear of actual or potential disorder. Elizabeth had to deal with subversion at court (Essex's quest for power), rebellions in Ireland and the north of England, and the constant threat of invasion from Spain. When Shakespeare gives his fullest and most systematic statement of the doctrine of cosmic hierarchy, he does so in *Troilus and Cressida*, a play which illustrates not the maintenance of order but a descent into egoistic anarchy.

Shakespeare's patrons included not only the monarchy but also court-iers like Essex and Southampton who were capable of conspiring against the Queen;[10] they included lawyers, scholars, shopkeepers, porters, cob-blers and waiters. Commentators on Shakespeare's plays and their back-ground are sometimes tempted to underestimate the diversity of beliefs and attitudes in the public, and thus to underestimate the volatility and openness of the texts. That *Measure for Measure* should have received a multiplicity of rival interpretations is not surprising; and what is always predictable is that each commentator tends to concentrate on advocacy of his or her single interpretation, instead of fully recognizing those features of the play and of cultural history which so bountifully beget 'a generation of still-breeding thoughts'. Those features include Shakespe-are's densely metaphoric poetry, the unpredictabilities of plot and charac-terization, and the textual lacunae; and, naturally, they include the commentators' customary vanity and ideological prejudice. Even today, commentary is haunted by the ghost of Sir Thomas Elyot's 'hierarchies' and 'degrees': 'in euery thyng is ordre, and without ordre may be nothing stable or permanent'. That ghost is diminished, though not exorcized, by Kenneth Muir's pronouncement on the plays: 'we can make statements about them which seem contradictory, and yet both express some aspect of the truth'.[11]

2.2 Approximate Chronology of Shakespeare's Works

The table in this section indicates the approximate dates of composition of Shakespeare's works. The word 'approximate' must be emphasized, since nobody knows for certain the precise date of composition of any one of the works. In the case of *Henry V*, the combination of internal evidence (e.g. the reference by the Chorus to Essex's Irish campaign) and external evidence (publication in 1600) makes it very likely that the play was written in 1599; but in other cases there is a dearth of useful evidence, and dating may be based on stylistic and thematic resemblances to other works of Shakespeare. Such a dearth makes highly conjectural the chronological locations of numerous plays, notably *The Taming of the Shrew*, *The Merry Wives of Windsor*, *Timon of Athens* and *Coriolanus*. My chronology is based on a comparison of various scholars' estimates, and I have given particular consideration to the evidence marshalled by the Arden editors.

In the following table, 'M' refers to the list of Shakespeare's works given by Francis Meres in his *Palladis Tamia: Wit's Treasury* (1598). 'P' refers to the earliest performance mentioned. A query after the letter P indicates that there is some doubt that the play mentioned by contemporaries is indeed Shakespeare's play or that it was indeed performed. 'Q' indicates the date of publication of the first Quarto text of a work. 'R' indicates the date of registration. In the heading '9½ Histories', the '½' refers to *Henry VIII*, for various scholars believe that this play was written jointly by Shakespeare and John Fletcher. Similarly, in the heading '16½ Comedies', the '½' refers to *The Two Noble Kinsmen*, which again is frequently thought to be a product of collaboration with Fletcher. Other texts which appear to include non-Shakespearian writing are *Titus Andronicus* and *Pericles*.

Although there is continuing debate about the dates and order of various Shakespearian texts, the sequences and layout of the table represent a reasonable 'working consensus'. Even when considerable allowance is made for chronological alternatives, the story told by the broad pattern of distribution of the works is in various ways instructive. If we look across the table at the earliest works in the various generic columns, it appears that the young Shakespeare had nerve, verve and cheek. The sheer range of those early works implies a pugnacious generic virtuosity: Shakespeare seems to be challenging predecessors and rivals in a wide variety of genres. As if to out-do contemporaneous revenge dramatists, he offers in *Titus Andronicus* the most spectacularly gory and horrific of revenge dramas. Sage chronicle–history plays were popular: and Shakespeare offers a whole trilogy on the reign of one king, Henry VI. To demonstrate his cunning in the field of farcical comedy, he takes a Plautine comedy, *Menaechmi*, which had *one* pair of identical twins, and with insolent dexterity multiplies the possibilities for farcical confusion by using *two* pairs in his version, *The Comedy of Errors*. Marlowe's *Hero and Leander* had offered a sensuous verse-narrative on a classical subject; and, as though to challenge Marlowe, Shakespeare produces *Venus and Adonis* and follows it with *The Rape of Lucrece*. The posthumous publication in 1591 of Sidney's *Astrophil and Stella* had quickened interest in the possibilities of the amatory sonnet-sequence; and, within a year or so, Shakespeare appears to have begun his own sequence, which in its story (of intense love for a beautiful youth and of intense lust for a courtesan) was and remains startlingly unconventional. The sense that Shakespeare was studying rival authors ('Desiring this man's art, and that man's scope'),[12] learning from them and boldly challenging them, is evoked not only by the rapid range and diversity of his works, not only by their profusion of borrowings from authors ancient and modern (Ovid, Seneca, Virgil, Plautus, Chaucer, Gower, Sidney, Kyd, Marlowe), but also by the critical references of contemporaries to his versatility and fertility – 'an absolute *Iohannes fac totum*'; 'hee flow'd with that facility, that sometime it was necessary he should be stop'd'.[13]

The table's generic division of the plays into 'Tragedies', 'Histories' and 'Comedies' maintains the tradition established by Shakespeare's colleagues when arranging his texts for the First Folio. The division is useful, but Shakespeare's imagination was adept at crossing frontiers of different kinds. It can be argued that *Julius Caesar*, though classified as a tragedy, has more in common with a history like *Richard II* than with a tragedy like *Romeo and Juliet*, and that *Richard III*, though classified as a history, has more in common with the tragedy *Macbeth* than with the history *Henry V*. Within the three nominal genres, various groups (sometimes overlapping) can be seen. Among the tragedies there is a group of five plays dealing with Graeco-Roman history and legend, an overlapping group featuring pairs of doomed lovers, and, overlapping the Graeco-Roman group, a trio of plays strongly related to the tradition of revenge drama (*Titus Andronicus*, *Hamlet* and *Othello*). Within the histories there are two evident tetralogies, the first extending from *1 Henry VI* to *Richard III*, the second consisting of *Richard II*, *1* and *2 Henry IV* and *Henry V*. Within the comedies, one very distinct group is that of the four late romances (*Pericles*, *Cymbeline*, *The Winter's Tale* and *The Tempest*). Since the 1890s, various critics have postulated a genre (the 'problem play') which overrides the nominal distinction between tragedy

Approximate Chronology of
(KEY: M = mentioned by Meres in 1598; P = performance;

11 TRAGEDIES	9½ HISTORIES
1590 *Titus Andronicus*: P 1592; R 1594; M.	⎰ *1 Henry VI*: P 1592.
	⎱ *2 Henry VI*: R 1594; Q 1594.
1	⎰ *3 Henry VI*: P by 1592; Q 1595.
	⎱ *Richard III*: P(?) 1593; R 1597; Q 1597; M.
2	
3	*King John*: M.
4	
1595 *Romeo and Juliet*: P by 1597; Q 1597; M.	*Richard II*: P 1595; R 1597; Q 1597; M.
6	
7	⎰ *1 Henry IV*: M(?); R 1598; Q 1598.
	⎱ *2 Henry IV*: M(?); R 1600; Q 1600.
8	
9 *Julius Caesar*: P by 1599.	*Henry V*: R(?) 1600; Q 1600.
1600 *Hamlet*: P 1602; R 1602; Q 1603.	
1	
2 *Troilus and Cressida*: R 1603; Q 1609.	
3	
4 *Othello*: P 1604.	
1605 *King Lear*: P 1606; R 1607; Q 1608.	
6 *Macbeth*: P 1611.	
7 *Antony and Cleopatra*: R 1608.	
8 *Timon of Athens. Coriolanus.*	
9	
1610	
11	
12	
13	*Henry VIII* (with Fletcher): P 1613.

Shakespeare's Works
Q = Quarto publication; R = registration.)

	16½ COMEDIES	POEMS
1590	{ *The Comedy of Errors*: P 1594; M. { *The Taming of the Shrew*: P(?) 1594.	
1		
2		
3	*The Two Gentlemen of Verona*: M.	*Venus and Adonis*: R 1593; Q 1593.
4		*The Rape of Lucrece*: R 1594; Q 1594.
1595	*Love's Labour's Lost*: P 1597(?); Q 1598; M.	(Between 1591 and 1600): *The Sonnets*:
6	*A Midsummer Night's Dream*: M.	M; sonnets 138 and 144: Q 1599;
7	*The Merchant of Venice*: R 1598; M.	all sonnets: Q 1609.
8	{ *The Merry Wives of Windsor*: P by 1602; R 1602; Q 1602. { *Much Ado About Nothing*: P by 1600; R 1600; Q 1600.	
9	*As You Like It*: R 1600.	
1600		
1	*Twelfth Night*: P 1602.	
2		
3	*All's Well That Ends Well.*	
4	*Measure for Measure*: P 1604.	
1605		
6		
7		
8	*Pericles*: R 1608; Q 1609.	
9	*Cymbeline*: P 1611.	
1610	*The Winter's Tale*: P 1611.	
11	*The Tempest*: P. 1611.	
12		
13	*The Two Noble Kinsmen*: P(?) 1619.	

and comedy by linking *Troilus and Cressida* (and perhaps *Hamlet*) with *All's Well That Ends Well* and *Measure for Measure*.

One of the virtues of the table is that it graphically shows how Shakespeare's interests evolve, partly in response to changing tastes in his audiences and partly in response to his inner imaginative needs. Before 1599 Shakespeare maintains a large output of histories and comedies, but seems relatively uninterested in tragedy. After 1599 there is a remarkable shift. The output of histories ceases as he concentrates intensively on a powerful sequence of tragedies. Almost simultaneously, the flow of exuberantly joyful comedies ceases: between 1601 and 1608 the only comedies are the relatively sombre and problematic *All's Well That Ends Well* and *Measure for Measure*; and it is tempting to imagine that while he was writing these two plays his main imaginative allegiance was engaged with those problems of suffering, death and justice which are traditionally the basis of tragedy. Then, as the great sequence of tragedies is completed, the 'late romances' emerge. One way of explaining the distinctive imaginative features of those romances from *Pericles* to *The Tempest* is to consider that they offer a consolatory solution to the problems of tragedy. One partial vindication of tragic suffering and death is this: that though the good may suffer and perish, the suffering is sometimes therapeutic, teaching valuable moral lessons or releasing new wisdom and eloquence. In the late romances it is almost as though Shakespeare thought: 'Yes, but how much better it would be if, when suffering and apparent death have taught their lessons, the suffering could be made good by new happiness and the apparently dead brought to life – here on earth. And is it not possible to imagine a new and better religion which is a synthesis of the most attractive features of Christianity and classical theology: which preserves the Christian emphasis on penitence, mercy and forgiveness, while permitting resurrection in *this* world; and which retains the pagan sense of deities moving on earth and associated with the bounty of the seasonal cycle, while rescinding the Ovidian sense of the carnal amorality of the classical gods and goddesses?' In their strange fusions and confusions of the Christian, the classical and the pastoral, the late romances regenerate mythology and provide an imaginative solution to those problems of tragedy which had been presented at their most bleak and uncompromising in *King Lear*.

If, as is very likely, *The Tempest* is the last of the plays which are written solely by Shakespeare, then his career as dramatist has a remarkably appropriate conclusion. *The Tempest* is in many ways retrospective. What is probably his first comedy, *The Comedy of Errors*, had combined with that farcical inner plot derived from Plautus a poignantly mythoid outer narrative derived from Gower's *Confessio Amantis*: a story of a family sundered at a time of storm and tempest, yet eventually reunited. *The Tempest* recapitulates and expands that situation and that thematic material. Again, *The Comedy of Errors* had maintained an unusually taut formal unity, approaching a neoclassical unity of place and preserving a neoclassical unity of time. In *The Tempest*, in stark contrast to the geographical and chronological vagrancy of *The Winter's Tale*, Shakespeare returns again to the formal tautness of *The Comedy of Errors*, the location being restricted to the island and its coast, and the time-sequence being conspicuously limited to four hours, from 2 p.m. to 6 p.m. Furthermore, it has often been noted that *The Tempest* has a resonantly retrospective, autobiographical quality. Prospero, completing his 'art', his sequence of magical transformations, determines to break his staff and drown his book in order to retire to the mainland; while Shakespeare was bringing to a close his own career as a transforming artist in order to retire to Stratford. Prospero says:

> graves at my command
> *Have wak'd their sleepers, op'd, and let 'em forth*
> *By my so potent art. But this rough magic*
> *I here abjure . . . . .*
>
> (V. i. 48–51)

And Shakespeare, too, had opened graves and waked their sleepers, giving new life to a Richard II, a Julius Caesar, an Antony, a Cleopatra, in a mimicry of the divine power to resurrect; Shakespeare too, veering between pride, self-criticism and possibly guilt, had been able to regard his own creativity both as 'my so potent art' and as 'this rough magic'. Furthermore, readers who believe that *Measure for Measure* expresses a profoundly Christian sensibility should reflect on that great speech of Prospero's which is the culmination of Shakespeare's long preoccupation with the relationship between death, sleep and dreams:

> *Our revels now are ended. These our actors,*
> *As I foretold you, were all spirits, and*
> *Are melted into air, into thin air;*
> *And, like the baseless fabric of this vision,*
> *The cloud-capp'd towers, the gorgeous palaces,*
> *The solemn temples, the great globe itself,*
> *Yea, all which it inherit, shall dissolve,*
> *And, like this insubstantial pageant faded,*
> *Leave not a rack behind. We are such stuff*
> *As dreams are made on; and our little life*
> *Is rounded with a sleep. Sir, I am vex'd . . . . .*
>
> (IV. i.148–58)

27

My magic, Prospero explains to Ferdinand, is entirely natural. You should not be surprised that you have just witnessed a magical transformation, since the entire creation is one great process of transformation; it is all one cosmic vanishing-act. However solid, big and durable any entities may appear, they are all decaying, dwindling and fading to nothing; and we, too, are part of this universe of dissolution, for we are but dream-stuff fading into sleep.

The source of the passage's beauty is also the source of its melancholy. Things distinct and massive blur and blend into shimmering, intangible evanescence: thin air, clouds, dreams, oblivion. Prospero has exalted the status of his magic, which is in harmony with a universe of transformation; but he has done so by dissolving the substantial status of the universe in which, here for a brief while, he has striven to effect a local regeneration by this magic. The source of his power dispels the results of that power and dispels even itself. Perhaps that is one of the reasons for Prospero's 'Sir, I am vex'd'. Like the 'solemn temples', the traditional consolations of religion – the assurance of an enduring otherworld, of an ultimate awakening from death's sleep into eternal life – have themselves dissolved and faded, and leave not a rack behind.

The relevance to *Measure for Measure* of this chronological survey may be summed up, then, as follows. The play clearly belongs to a transitional phase in Shakespeare's career, and the direction of that transition was from histories and comedies to tragedies. This provides some contextual support for those commentators who feel that in *Measure for Measure* Shakespeare's imaginative powers are far more strongly evoked by the grim dilemmas of the action than by the devices culminating in the happy ending. Towards the end of his career, in those late romances, Shakespeare resumes the themes of regeneration, reconciliation and the reunion of families which he had deliberately incorporated in the early *Comedy of Errors* and which were still important in *Measure for Measure* (indeed Duke Vincentio partly anticipates Prospero), but now Shakespeare draws strongly on elements of myth or magic to strengthen the force of the happy dénouement. Aided by white magic, by Ariel and an enchanted island, Prospero needs no monk's disguise and wiles of impersonation. Lastly, the quality of plangent cosmic scepticism in Prospero's meditation on 'this insubstantial pageant faded' shows that, though Shakespeare frequently gave powerful imaginative expression to various concepts closely associated with New Testament Christianity, he was also capable of giving imaginative assent to non-Christian eschatologies, and this should be borne in mind when Christian interpretations of *Measure for Measure* are considered.

2.21 *The Date of* Measure for Measure

The Revels Accounts state that 'Mesur for Mesur' by 'Shaxberd' was performed in the banqueting hall at Court on 26 December 1604; and probably it was earlier in the same year that the play was written. To establish this probability, editors have postulated a variety of topical allusions in the text; and even if the reader does not accept all their postulates, the background material thus adduced does emphasize the potential for topicalities in the social and political content of the play.

In I.ii.85–9, Pompey refers to 'the proclamation' that 'All houses in the suburbs of Vienna must be plucked down'. On 16 September 1603, as a precaution against the continued spread of the plague, a royal proclamation had called for the pulling down of a number of houses in the suburbs of London: various brothels and gambling dens were closed and demolished. In IV.iii.14–20, Pompey remarks that the jail now holds several fighters or brawlers known to him; and street-brawling in London had been curbed by a 'Statute of Stabbing' passed between March and July 1604. In I.ii.75–7, Mistress Overdone complains:

Thus, what with the war, what with the sweat, what with the gallows, and what with poverty, I am custom-shrunk.

J. W. Lever says that this complaint 'links a number of factors operative in the winter of 1603–4: the continuance of the war with Spain; the plague in London; the treason trials and executions . . . . . ; the slackness of trade in the deserted capital'.[14]

The play may also contain various allusions to King James, who, on Queen Elizabeth's death in 1603, had travelled from Scotland to London for his accession to the English throne. In *Measure for Measure*, I.i.67–72, the Duke remarks that he himself is reluctant to appear in public because he does not like the 'loud applause and *Aves* vehement' of the crowd; and a similar reluctance was a noted feature of James's conduct, as contemporary chroniclers recalled. Sir Roger Wilbraham reported that when the new King first arrived in London, he proceeded to visit parts of the city 'secretlie in his coach and by water'. Wilson's *Life and Reign of James I* stated:

The King's first going abroad [i.e. venturing out in London] was privately to visit some of his Houses, for naturally he did not love to be looked on . . . . . [W]hen he came abroad, he was so troubled with Swarms, that he fear'd to be baited by the People . . . . . [I]n his publick Appearances (especially in his Sports) the Accesses of the People made him so impatient, that he often dispersed them with Frowns, that we may not say with Curses . . . .

And D'Ewes's *Autobiography* said that James 'often, in his sudden distemper, would bid a p[ox] or plague on such as flocked to see him'.[15]

In II.iv.20–30, Angelo observes that when

> *The general subject to a well-wish'd king*
> *Quit their own part, and in obsequious fondness*
> *Crowd to his presence,*

they may unwittingly offend him, resembling a foolish throng which, gathering around a man who has swooned, deprives him unintentionally of the air he needs. In the middle of March 1604, King James had attempted to pay a secret visit to the Exchange, but the crowds had recognized him and pressed closely upon him before they could be shut out. This caused him offence, given that in Scotland his subjects preferred to 'stand still, see all, and vse silence'. His discomfiture was reported in *The Time Triumphant* (registered in March 1604), a tract whose authorship was claimed by Robert Armin, a member of Shakespeare's company of players.[16]

These possible allusions (coupled with the play's style, its resemblances to *All's Well That Ends Well*, and the record of a performance in December of that year) suggest that *Measure for Measure* may well have been written in the summer of 1604. The theatres had been closed during 1603 because of the plague but re-opened in April 1604, so there may have been public performances at the Globe Theatre before the recorded performance at Whitehall.

Measure for Measure contains substantial discussion of the qualities required of a good ruler, so the play could readily be deemed to have some reference to James, who had acceded to the throne in the previous year (and who had become the titular patron of Shakespeare's company). The Duke takes an attentively active part in practical politics and is also described as a philosopher in temperament: he is 'One that, above all other strifes, contended especially to know himself . . . . A gentleman of all temperance' (III.ii.226–7, 231). (Plato's *Protagoras* said that the temple of Apollo at Delphi was inscribed with the wise and famous sayings, 'Know thyself' and 'Nothing in extremes'.) King James prided himself on being a scholarly philosopher as well as an active political leader. In *Basilikon Doron* (first published in Edinburgh in 1599, in London in 1603) he wrote that a person's good qualities should not be harboured inwardly but should be set to public work – the advice offered by the Duke to Angelo in I.i.29–40 – and that even an admirable ruler may be the victim of slanders by 'the common people'. He certainly commended temperance. Just possibly, one factor which led Shakespeare to the title of his play was

James's advice to his son: 'And aboue all, let the measure of your loue to euery one, be according to the measure of his vertue.'[17]

Shakespeare was undoubtedly capable of making flattering reference, within a play, to a reigning monarch. *A Midsummer Night's Dream*, II.i.155–64, contains what is almost certainly a tribute to Queen Elizabeth ('a fair vestal, thronèd by the west'). *Macbeth* is generally believed to have been occasioned by the accession to the English throne of King James VI of Scotland. The belief is supported particularly by the play's elaborate depiction of the manifold virtues of Malcolm, James's precursor, and by its account of the long line of Banquo's royal successors which includes an 'eighth king' who will unite two kingdoms and have an extensive royal posterity. Furthermore, its presentation of the three witches would have won approval from the monarch who, in his *Daemonologie* (1597), had cited the Bible to support his contentions that witches really existed and wielded hellish powers. Nevertheless, most of the postulated specific linkages between King James and the Duke of *Measure for Measure* are questionable. James may have been offended by the harrying crowd at the Exchange, but in plays written before his accession various rulers (Henry IV, Richard II and Julius Caesar, for example)[18] had expressed a patrician distaste for the common multitude. And James's dislike of slanderers, and his advocacy of temperance and active virtue, are not notably original: both he and Shakespeare's Duke are expressing traditional commonplaces which can be traced back to the Bible (or, for that matter, to Homer, Virgil and Seneca). Nevertheless, on balance, it seems a probability that some analogies between Duke Vincentio and King James intermittently entered Shakespeare's imagination.

The most interesting connections are perhaps these. At Newark in April 1603, James sentenced a cutpurse to immediate death (without trial) but simultaneously amnestied most of the prisoners in the Castle:[19] an act which brings to mind the startling inquiry about Barnardine in IV.ii.130–32: 'How came it that the absent Duke had not either delivered him to his liberty, or executed him? I have heard it was ever his manner to do so.' And at Winchester in the winter of 1603–4 a number of condemned conspirators against the King were taken to the scaffold but then told that they had been reprieved, James having arranged for the announcement of the reprieve to be delayed until they had suffered the agony of believing that their execution was imminent.[20] This shows that a partial historical warrant could be cited for one of the most 'theatrical' elements of Act V: the Duke's cat-and-mouse game with Angelo, who is allowed to think that his execution is inevitable before the Duke mercifully intercedes.

The play shows the hypocritically cruel misrule of the Puritanical

Angelo and appears to vindicate the more humane justice of the Duke. In January 1604 the King had been chairman of a conference at Hampton Court between representatives of the Puritans and of the Bishops; James offered some concessions to the Puritans but made clear his hostility to the political threat they represented: 'I shall make them conforme themselves, or I wil harrie them out of the land, or else doe worse.'[21] In *Measure for Measure* can be glimpsed some features of a consolatory political myth: that the dangerous rectitude and severity of the Puritans may eventually be contained and held in subordination by a vigilant and resourceful ruler. The reality, as James's son, Charles, was to learn at the executioner's block, would be harsher. We may, however, recall that myth while we read those verse-tributes in which Ben Jonson claims that Shakespeare's writings 'so did take *Eliza*, and our *Iames*!'[22]

While the Puritans advanced against the monarchy, they also advanced against secular folk-traditions. If we accept that *Measure for Measure* was written in 1604, we may see the topicality of its depiction of two lovers who find that their private marriage-contract is both sinful and unlawful. On the continent, at the Council of Trent (1545–63), the Roman Catholic Church had decreed that the presence of a priest was necessary if a marriage were to be valid and binding. In England, the Anglican Church had continued to regard private betrothals as lawful; but in 1604, largely in response to pressure from the Puritans, the ecclesiastical courts endorsed reforms which brought their practice closer to that of the civil courts, which recognized only church weddings.[23] A subsequent instance of the increasing ecclesiastical hostility to the centuries-old custom of private spousals is provided by the records of Stratford, cited by Edgar I. Fripp:

On 27 July 1622, Michael Palmer and his wife Jane were presented at Stratford by the churchwardens as having acknowledged with penitence 'their incontinency before marriage and their offence in being married without banns or licence', and 'promised from henceforth they will live as Christians ought to do'. Their child, Thomas, had been baptized on 28 April, and being the offspring of contracted parents, was not marked 'notus', 'spurius', or 'bastard'.[24]

Had they seen Claudio or Juliet of *Measure for Measure*, Michael and Jane would have been forewarned about the encroachment of authority on the ancient domain of private and secular spousals.

2.3 The Sonnets and *Measure for Measure*

In the 1590s, after the publication of Sidney's *Astrophil and Stella* in 1591, Elizabethans vied with each other in writing amatory sonnet-sequences. Samuel Daniel's *Delia* sequence appeared in 1592, and its preface offers a handsome tribute to Sidney's *Astrophil*. Michael Drayton's *Idea* was published in 1594, Spenser's *Amoretti* in 1595; and there were numerous others. Commentators differ about the dates of composition of Shakespeare's sonnets (Leslie Hotson ascribes them to the 1580s), but the general view is that they were written between 1591 and 1600. Conspicuous parallels to features in the sonnets can be found in *Venus and Adonis* and *The Rape of Lucrece* (published in 1593 and 1594) and in three plays believed to have been written around 1595: *Romeo and Juliet*, *Richard II* and *Love's Labour's Lost*. In *Romeo and Juliet*, the first exchange of dialogue between the two lovers forms a perfect Shakespearian sonnet: fourteen lines, rhyming A B A B C B C B D E D E F F. *Richard II* contains much conspicuously ingenious, 'conceited' verse, the punning on the name of Gaunt bringing to mind the sonnets which pun on 'Will' and 'Hews'. In *Love's Labour's Lost*, various characters vie in producing amatory sonnets (though not all strictly in sonnet form), and Berowne's ingenious defence of his Rosaline's dark beauty (IV.iii.254–61) repeats the logic of sonnet 127. Particularly interesting is that when, at the end of Act III scene i, Berowne bitterly complains that he loves

> *A whitely wanton with a velvet brow,*
> *With two pitch balls stuck in her face for eyes;*
> *Ay, and by heaven, one that will do the deed,*
> *Though Argus were her eunuch and her guard*

– when he says that, his tone and terms bring to mind sonnets 137, 141 and 147; indeed, he seems to be thinking of the 'dark lady' of the sonnets rather than of the Rosaline of *Love's Labour's Lost*, for though Rosaline is quite capable of bawdy innuendoes there is nothing in the play to suggest that she is a courtesan who 'will do the deed,/Though Argus were her eunuch'. It is as though, for a moment, Berowne had become a spokesman for the bitter experiences recorded in the sonnets, and a discrepancy appears between his feelings and his dramatic context. Perhaps some of the sonnet-experiences, by inducing states of inner division and moral ambiguity, helped to push Shakespeare the dramatist in the direction of greater realism and towards the so-called 'problem plays'.

In 1598 Francis Meres referred to Shakespeare's 'sugred Sonnets among his priuate friends';[25] and in 1599 two of the sonnets which appear to come late in the narrative sequence (numbers 138 and 144) were published in a collection called *The Passionate Pilgrim*. This makes it likely that the sequence as a whole was completed a decade before its appearance in the First Quarto of 1609 and well before the publication of *Measure for Measure*.

In the fourteenth century, Chaucer's Troilus had plagiarized the love-laments of Petrarch,[26] and his rapturous passivity had been astutely mocked by Pandarus. Already Petrarch and the poets of courtly love had established those conventions and clichés of situation, attitude and expression which were to sustain amatory sonneteers for the following three hundred years. Traditionally in such poems, the lover is a man who adores a beautiful, virtuous and largely inaccessible young woman. He blazons her beauty and apotheosizes her virtue; he experiences yearning desire, hope and despair; his love for her is a living death, a freezing fire, a blissful torment. In Chaucer, and later in Wyatt and Sidney, the harmonies of romantic hyperbole were often accompanied by the deliberate discords of scepticism and cynicism: there could be grudging, rebellious, self-mocking notes. Yet for all the diversity of the tradition, there was no precedent for the narrative boldness of Shakespeare's sonnets.

Shakespeare's sequence has been famous so long, quoted and recited in schools and colleges around the world, that the daring of its story has become veiled by familiarity. The fact remains that most of his love-sonnets are addressed, in defiance of convention, to a man and not a woman; that they express no mere platonized Renaissance patron-worship but a love which is strongly sexual in its range, terms, jealousies; and that those sonnets which do address a woman address no paragon of beauty and virtue but (in 144 and 137) 'a woman colour'd ill' who is 'the bay where all men ride'. It's true that a few of the sonnets are merely literary exercises, ingenious variations on ancient literary topics: for example, sonnets 153 and 154, which develop the conceits of Marianus about Cupid's burning torch. But in the main the sequence appears to be strongly autobiographical. This is what we should expect: for Petrarch's Laura really existed, and so did Spenser's Elizabeth; as indeed, in the 1940s, did John Berryman's Lise. Furthermore, Shakespeare's sonnet-narrative often displays a commentator-thwarting obscurity and privacy of allusion which are exactly what one would expect to occur when a body of poetry is addressed primarily to a real recipient who is involved in a continuing relationship on which the poems comment.

There is scholarly disagreement about the correct order of Shakespeare's sonnets, and their story is partly cryptic and jumbled. But what still emerges clearly is the most odd and interesting story of any English sonnet-sequence. The story is this. Shakespeare has apparently been commissioned by an aristocratic family to write poems to persuade the son of that family to marry and thus beget an heir. You're very beautiful, says the poet, but you mustn't let that beauty die out: you must take a wife and defeat time by breeding living copies of your beauty. But then the poet appears to betray his commission. Instead of saying that the young Adonis should gain immortality through offspring, he says that the poet loves him deeply and can immortalize him through his poetry. Their relationship develops in the course of three years: the writer is now ecstatic and confident, now jealous and reproachful. The 'lovely boy' can appear decadent, aloof, coldblooded; rivals, including a rival poet, attract his favours; Shakespeare, socially inferior, fascinated and obsessed, can experience a bitter sense that the young man may be morally duplicitous and treacherous. And in the sonnets to the 'dark lady', there is again an oscillation and entanglement of emotion: she can be seen as beautiful and ugly, an enchantress and a whore. Even the rise and fall of the penis in sexual intercourse can then be sensed, in sardonic punning, as a self-betraying drudgery which evokes the original pride and fall of erring humanity:

> For thou betraying me, I do betray
> My nobler part to my gross body's treason;
> My soul doth tell my body that he may
> Triumph in love; flesh stays no farther reason,
> But, rising at thy name, doth point out thee
> As his triumphant prize. Proud of this pride,
> He is contented thy poor drudge to be,
> To stand in thy affairs, fall by thy side.
>   No want of conscience hold it that I call
>   Her 'love' for whose dear love I rise and fall.
>   (151, lines 5–14)

To make matters worse, there is multiple treachery: apparently the 'dark lady' has seduced the young man:

> To win me soon to hell, my female evil
> Tempteth my better angel from my side,
> And would corrupt my saint to be a devil,
> Wooing his purity with her foul pride.
> And whether that my angel be turn'd fiend,
> Suspect I may, yet not directly tell;
> But being both from me, both to each friend,
> I guess one angel in another's hell . . . . .
>   (144, lines 5–12)

35

And the treachery is all along compounded by the poet, a man forsworn: a husband and a father, who professes undying love for a lascivious aristocrat and proclaims his servitude to a black-haired adulteress. There is extreme tension within the sonnets between love seen as supremely exalting, a time-defying mutuality, and love seen as the corruption of moral judgement by lustful infatuation. Some of the poems have a blasphemous edge; whereas one (146: 'Poor soul, the centre of my sinful earth') is a staunchly Christian exhortation to attain Heaven through asceticism. Some are majestic, some richly lyrical, some trivial, and others arcanely ambiguous. In *Measure for Measure*, it is as though Shakespeare could give analytic distribution, amplification and dialectical clarification to the complex, contradictory and sometimes blurred feelings that the sonnets express; and if the clarification was not always complete, that was because some terms, the sexual and the ascetic, so powerfully evoked contradictory associations.

It is easy enough to relate the *contemptus mundi* argument of sonnet 146 to the Duke's 'Be absolute for death . . . . .' in I I I.i.5–41, to hear echoes of the bawdy punning of 151 in the speeches of Lucio and Pompey, or to see connections between the fall of Angelo and the imagery of the corruptible 'angel' in 144. The most fruitfully relevant sonnets are probably 129 and 94.

> *Th'expense of spirit in a waste of shame*
> *Is lust in action; and till action, lust*
> *Is perjur'd, murd'rous, bloody, full of blame,*
> *Savage, extreme, rude, cruel, not to trust;*
> *Enjoy'd no sooner but despisèd straight;*
> *Past reason hunted, and, no sooner had,*
> *Past reason hated, as a swallowed bait,*
> *On purpose laid to make the taker mad –*
> *Mad in pursuit, and in possession so;*
> *Had, having, and in quest to have, extreme;*
> *A bliss in proof, and prov'd, a very woe;*
> *Before, a joy propos'd; behind, a dream.*
>   *All this the world well knows; yet none knows well*
>   *To shun the heaven that leads men to this hell.*

> (129)

Much of the action of *Measure for Measure* could be regarded as an explanatory elaboration of the sonnet's rapid, epigrammatic yet feverishly intense definition of 'lust in action'. The conduct of Angelo amply shows how lust can be 'perjur'd, murd'rous', 'Savage, extreme', 'Past reason hunted' and 'Past reason hated'. More important is the connection between lines 6 to 10 of the sonnet and the words of Claudio to Lucio near the beginning of the play. Lust is likened in those lines to 'a swallowed bait,/On purpose laid to make the taker mad –/Mad in pursuit, and in possession so'. In Act I, scene ii, Lucio says to Claudio, who is being led to prison, 'Whence comes this restraint?'; and Claudio replies:

> *From too much liberty, my Lucio. Liberty,*
> *As surfeit, is the father of much fast;*
> *So every scope by the immoderate use*
> *Turns to restraint. Our natures do pursue,*
> *Like rats that ravin down their proper bane,*
> *A thirsty evil; and when we drink, we die.*

Lucio subsequently inquires whether Claudio's offence is 'lechery', and receives the reply: 'Call it so.' Yet Claudio then proceeds to explain that the relationship between Juliet and himself, far from being one of lechery, is marital: 'upon a true contract/I got possession of Julietta's bed'. They are wife and husband according to a secular marriage-contract and had fully intended that the marriage should eventually be consecrated in church; but meantime Juliet has become pregnant and the two have fallen foul of the re-activated old law against fornication, according to which (evidently) a secular marriage-contract is both sinful and unlawful. There is no doubt that Claudio and Juliet are a loving couple who had every intention of living together as husband and wife. The strange anomaly, then, is the vigour and intensity of Claudio's depiction of himself as one to whom liberty and sexuality have been as rat-poison, a lethal 'thirsty evil'. The image is intensely pejorative: it suggests a base, greedy, stupid appetite for what seems delectable but is in reality lethally destructive. Claudio has good grounds to feel indignant at the inappropriate application of a ruthless law; instead, he seems to be vindicating the law by seeing himself not as virtual husband but as ravenous pest. Rat-bait had the effect of inducing an avid thirst in its devourer; and when the rodent next drank, the combination of water and the poison killed it. This poison is clearly the 'swallowed bait' of the sonnet as well as the 'proper bane' (appropriate poison) mentioned by Claudio. (A related image-cluster is found in sonnet 118.) It is Lucio, not Claudio, who describes the couple's love and Juliet's pregnancy as a matter of 'tilth and husbandry', of bounty natural as harvest.

The Provost takes a fairly liberal view: he describes Claudio as 'a young man/More fit to do another such offence,/Than die for this' (II.iii.13–15). To Escalus, the 'fault' is venial. Yet it is not Angelo alone who regards it as a sin deserving death: the Duke as Friar says 'It is too general a vice, and severity must cure it', and Juliet herself acquiesces in the judgement and even accepts the Duke's claim that since the act of sexual intercourse 'was mutually committed', her 'sin' is 'of heavier kind' than Claudio's. At the end of the play, of course, the Duke is happy to pronounce pardon on Claudio, though he still terms Juliet a person 'wrong'd' whom the young man must 'restore'.

Part of the difficulty is that nobody in the play fully and decisively makes the statement that the situation of Claudio and Juliet seems so obviously to solicit: the statement that a law which makes no distinction between hardened whores and a young betrothed couple aiming for holy wedlock is a law so crassly indiscriminate that it should be repealed. But if the play had included a vigorous denunciatory speech on these lines (perhaps from Escalus or Provost or Claudio or Juliet), this might have damaged the Duke's authority and reduced the ethical extremism on which the plot's tension depends. One source of the difficulty may be very personal to Shakespeare, in a way that the sonnets suggest. The ruthless law of the fictional Vienna could perhaps be sensed by him as one which derived some vindication from an experienced association of desire with self-treachery and entrapment. Or, to put it less speculatively, Shakespeare had good personal reason for associating the appetitive, in various forms, not only with nurture, procreation and harvest, but also with the voracious, subversive and morally destructive ('And appetite, an universal wolf . . . . . Must . . . . . last eat up himself'):[27] sexual disgust he had richly and variously known, and this prior embodied and imaged knowledge pressed readily into a receptive imagination as he – partly improvising, partly calculating – created the play. Perhaps the very inner copulation which generated the literary work was a tainted intercourse: 'And almost thence my nature is subdu'd/To what it works in', complained sonnet 111; Theseus had scornfully linked 'The lunatic, the lover and the poet'; and Prospero would eventually abjure 'this rough magic'.[28]

Sonnet 94 displays a cluster of ambiguous feelings which later find partial expression in the characterization of Angelo:

> *They that have power to hurt and will do none,*
> *That do not do the thing they most do show,*
> *Who, moving others, are themselves as stone,*
> *Unmovèd, cold, and to temptation slow –*
> *They rightly do inherit Heaven's graces,*
> *And husband nature's riches from expense;*
> *They are the lords and owners of their faces,*
> *Others but stewards of their excellence.*
> *The summer's flow'r is to the summer sweet*

> *Though to itself it only live and die;*
> *But if that flow'r with base infection meet,*
> *The basest weed outbraves his dignity.*
>   *For sweetest things turn sourest by their deeds:*
>   *Lilies that fester smell far worse than weeds.*

Taken out of context, this sonnet appears to offer a series of general reflections on a particular type of person; taken in context, it appears much more personal: a warning from the poet to the 'lovely boy'. In the sequence as traditionally numbered, the previous sonnet says that the young man looks constant and loving, but may yet be false:

> *How like Eve's apple doth thy beauty grow,*
> *If thy sweet virtue answer not thy show!*

And the subsequent sonnet, 95, says that his beautiful appearance and style seem to veil and even to render benign those vices which are reported to lie within him, though this privilege may not endure. So sonnet 94 then seems to be a warning to the young man, and the immediate nature of the warning appears to be quite clear: pride may come before a fall; *corruptio optimi pessima* – the corruption of the best is the worst kind of corruption. A slower reading reveals the ambiguities. The first line, 'They that have power to hurt and will do none', seems to evoke approval of those mentioned: it's surely good for powerful people not to inflict injury. The second line, 'That do not do the thing they most do show', is equivocal: to decline to wield a destructive power may be good, yet to be deceptive – to seem one thing and be another – may be bad. The next two lines are largely negative and partly positive:

> *Who, moving others, are themselves as stone,*
> *Unmovèd, cold, and to temptation slow . . . . .*

To be 'to temptation slow' seems better than to be to temptation quick, though not as good as being to temptation immune ('slow' implies the possibility of an eventual succumbing). However, the simile 'as stone,/Unmovèd, cold' has a strongly negative charge: it implies an almost inhumanly callous aloofness. The next couplet nevertheless asserts that such people have good warrant for their conduct:

> *They rightly do inherit Heaven's graces,*
> *And husband nature's riches from expense . . . . .*

It seems unequivocal; yet numerous earlier sonnets had stressed that good natural husbandry entails procreation rather than self-containment; to preserve oneself from sin may serve Heaven, but various biblical parables had said that talents given by God should be put to good use and not withheld. One parable that might seem to vindicate self-containment is that in Matthew VI, when Christ says: 'Learne, how the lilies of the field do growe: they labour not, nether spinne: Yet I say vnto you, That euen Solomon in all his glorie was not arayed like one of these'; and a memory of this passage may be moving under the surface of the sonnet to emerge in the subsequent flower imagery and the 'Lilies that fester' of the final line.[29] When we consider the subsequent statement –

> *They are the lords and owners of their faces,*
> *Others but stewards of their excellence*

– this, again, has a distinctly equivocal effect. Purportedly it is a vindication; yet the contrast between 'of their faces' and 'of their excellence' gives a fleeting impression that these powerful men are vacantly complacent, while the underlings, the 'stewards', are doing the real work. Then the ambivalence is clarified as the warning emerges. Some people may resemble flowers in their beauty, fragrance and self-containment, but, should they become corrupted, their corruption will be all the worse. The main source of the sonnet's ambiguity may be this contradiction in Shakespeare's feelings: if the young man is coldly aloof, that at least preserves him from sexual entanglements with Shakespeare's rivals; yet that cold aloofness from Shakespeare, though no doubt justifiable on social and moral grounds, can seem harsh to the loving poet; and the worst of all combinations would be coldness to the poet and warmth to rivals, which would seem hypocritical and treacherous. William Empson remarks: 'The fact that the feelings in this sonnet could be used for such different people as Angelo and Prince Henry, different both in their power and their coldness, is an essential part of its breadth.'[30]

The application to Angelo is clear. He is initially perceived as indeed 'Unmovèd, cold, and to temptation slow': his 'blood is very snow-broth', 'his urine is congealed ice'. The sonnet's assertion that such detached people rightly 'husband nature's riches from expense' meets its appropriate contradiction in the Duke's instruction to Angelo (I.i.36–40) that talents should be used:

> *nature never lends*
> *The smallest scruple of her excellence*
> *But, like a thrifty goddess, she determines*
> *Herself the glory of a creditor,*
> *Both thanks and use.*

The sonnet's image of the 'summer's flow'r' and the 'Lilies that fester' is evidently related to, though transformed in, Angelo's guilty soliloquy in II.ii.164–8:

> *The tempter, or the tempted, who sins most, ha?*
> *Not she; nor doth she tempt; but it is I*
> *That, lying by the violet in the sun,*
> *Do as the carrion does, not as the flower,*
> *Corrupt with virtuous season.*

Angelo deems himself to be paradoxically corrupted by virtue, tempted by the chaste Isabella as he never was by 'the strumpet/With all her double vigour'. In his metaphor, the sun is the source of virtue; the violet is Isabella, nurtured by virtue; and Angelo is the carrion which the sun's heat rots – made evil by what is good. The phrase 'virtuous season' is neatly ambiguous. It may refer to summer, the time of radiance and growth. It certainly invokes 'seasoning': whatever adds relish to foods: here the meat in the sun is seasoned or scented with the violet's fragrance.

Shakespeare had associated the sun with carrion and sexuality in *Hamlet* (II.ii.180–86):

For if the sun breed maggots in a dead dog, being a good kissing carrion - Have you a daughter? ....
Let her not walk i' th' sun. Conception is a blessing. But as your daughter may conceive – friend, look to't.

There may seem to be no carrion in sonnet 94, but the association of summer's sun, sexuality and flesh may have generated the particular force of the phrase 'Lilies that fester': since its force lies largely in the unexpectedness of that word 'fester', which (unlike, say, 'wither' or even 'decay') is normally applied specifically to flesh that can suppurate.

The main implication of this section can now be educed. In *Measure for Measure* Shakespeare used a considerable variety of source-material, some literary and traditional, some topical. There is evidence that around 1600 Elizabethan dramatists (Jonson, Marston, Dekker and others) responded to a popular demand for greater realism, and gave prominence to satiric material (particularly the satiric presentation of sexual vice and hypocrisy). It is also the case, however, that some of the most forceful and ambiguous passages in *Measure for Measure* have a clear relationship to certain of the sonnets; and the hypothesis that in the play Shakespeare was using some personal source-material, drawing imaginatively on the experiences recorded in (or formulated during) his sonnet-sequence, is plausible not only as a matter of aetiology but also as basis for elucidation of some of the play's ambiguities.

2.4 The 'Problem Plays'

Measure for Measure is one of those Shakespeare plays which numerous critics have found strangely troubling and perplexing, and in the late nineteenth century a particular group emerged as the 'problem plays'.

In 1686 John Dryden had dismissed the play as 'meanly written', and in 1765 Samuel Johnson anticipated many later commentators by saying: 'There is perhaps not one of *Shakespear*'s plays more darkened than this by the peculiarities of its Authour . . . . .' In the nineteenth century opinions were divided: Coleridge found the comic elements 'disgusting', the serious elements 'horrible', and deemed the whole 'a hateful work', while the radical Hazlitt respected the play's unconventional diversity and claimed that the author was 'a moralist in the same sense in which nature is one'. Later, Algernon Swinburne felt that the play belonged to a small group, 'not accurately definable', of 'tragedies docked of their natural end'.[31]

The action of *Measure for Measure* ends happily: perils are overcome, injustices rectified by a lenient poetic justice, and several couples are paired off in marriages; so the play is obviously a comedy rather than a tragedy. But the more conventional or superficial one's notion of comedy, the more unconventional *Measure for Measure* may seem; and various critics have felt that it requires a different generic term. Furthermore, there seemed to be some strange family-resemblances between *Measure for Measure* and three other plays which appeared between 1600 and 1604: *Hamlet*, *Troilus and Cressida* and *All's Well That Ends Well*. In all of them, sexuality, sexual disgust and bawdry have full and frank presentation; cynical spokesmen or cynical points of view are prominent; in all except *All's Well* moral and philosophical debate is sustained and strenuous; and in all four, neither the heroes nor the heroines fully gratify conventional expectations. Hamlet may be 'The courtier's, soldier's, scholar's, eye, tongue, sword', but his treatment of Ophelia is brutal and his dispatch of Polonius callous, while Ophelia is too much the hapless victim to seem a 'tragic heroine'. Troilus is appetitive, irrational, vengeful, while Cressida submits with a sigh to whoredom. Helena is ardently resourceful, but the immature and snobbish Bertram remains unworthy of her pursuit. Claudio can seem convincingly yet ignobly anguished, while Isabella's vehement rectitude is sometimes repellent. If, as a novelist, Charles Dickens can be accused of making it too easy for us to feel warmhearted to virtue and indignant against vice, in this group of plays Shakespeare (some critics claim) has made it confusingly difficult for us to do so. The currency of the term 'problem plays' for this group can be traced to George Bernard Shaw.

In the 1890s, Shaw, strongly influenced by Ibsen's social dramas, was keen to emphasize in his prefaces that various plays of his were important because they dealt with current social problems; and in the Preface to *Plays Unpleasant* (1898) he made the genially immodest connection between his own preoccupations and three of Shakespeare's plays. He remarked of Shakespeare: '[I]n such unpopular plays as All's Well, Measure for Measure, and Troilus and Cressida, we find him ready and willing to start at the twentieth century if the seventeenth would only let him.'[32]

The term 'problem play' had thus been given currency during the 1890s by the increasing popularity of the social dramas of Ibsen and Shaw; and it was F. S. Boas who transferred the term to *Hamlet, Troilus and Cressida, All's Well That Ends Well* and *Measure for Measure*. In his book, *Shakspere and His Predecessors* (1896), Boas explained:

All these dramas introduce us into highly artificial societies, whose civilization is ripe unto rottenness. Amidst such media abnormal conditions of brain and of emotion are generated, and intricate cases of conscience demand a solution by unprecedented methods. Thus throughout these plays we move along dim untrodden paths, and at the close our feeling is neither of simple joy nor pain; we are excited, fascinated, perplexed, for the issues raised preclude a completely satisfactory outcome, even when, as in *All's Well* and *Measure for Measure*, the complications are outwardly adjusted in the fifth act. In *Troilus and Cressida* and *Hamlet* no such partial settlement of difficulties takes place, and we are left to interpret their enigmas as best we may. Dramas so singular in theme and temper cannot be strictly called comedies or tragedies. We may therefore borrow a convenient phrase from the theatre of to-day and class them together as Shakspere's problem-plays.[33]

This passage is clearly related to the preoccupations of the 1890s. Not only have the controversial dramas of Ibsen and Shaw contributed the 'convenient phrase', but also the contemporaneous discussions (by Nordau, Wilde, Symons and many others) of modern 'decadence' and 'degeneration' are echoed in Boas's phrases: 'civilization ..... ripe unto rottenness'; 'abnormal conditions of brain and of emotion'. Boas has neatly overcome a generic difficulty: if it is a problem to know what to call a play (because it does not seem to fit conventional categories), what better solution than to call that kind of play a 'problem play'? And he clearly suggests that the generic problem has been caused by an internal problem: 'the issues raised preclude a completely satisfactory outcome'. This claim has been extremely influential: some critics have supported it and some have opposed it, but almost all have (explicitly or implicitly) referred to it.

Critics who, like Boas, feel that these four plays of the period 1600 to 1604 are characterized by decadent or morbid elements, and who are troubled by those elements, have sometimes sought to explain them by a biographical hypothesis. They have suggested that, at this period in his career, Shakespeare's mind was darkened by morbid, cynical, unhealthy feelings: the poet had evidently experienced a personal, emotional disillusionment. Proponents of this explanation include John Dover Wilson, Caroline Spurgeon and Una Ellis-Fermor. Spurgeon, for example, writes:

Just as a man with gnawing toothache takes pleasure in biting on the tooth, and thereby increasing the pain, so one feels in these plays that Shakespeare, whose deepest and purest feelings have somehow been sorely hurt, takes pleasure in hurting them still more by exposing all the horrible, revolting, perplexing and grotesque aspects of human nature . . . . . [T]here is ample evidence of a shocked, disillusioned and suffering spirit, taking refuge in mocks and jeers and bitterness.[34]

This biographical postulate, then, can be employed to 'excuse' or 'explain away' features in the plays which the critic finds disturbing or distressing: the author's spirit had been lacerated, and for a while he was deprived of his normal, healthy frame of mind. As we have seen, this postulate can be supported by reference to some of the later sonnets, with their intensity of sexual disgust and their bitter recognition of the ways in which sexual desire may subvert both the aesthetic and the moral judgement, luring the individual into multiple betrayals. Nevertheless, Spurgeon's case is partly hypothetical and circular; the more favourable a critic's view of these plays, the less pathological will be the explanation.

Another way of explaining or excusing the supposedly morbid features of this group of plays was the historical one. It could be argued that as the Elizabethan era gave way to the Jacobean, so the cultural climate changed: a sense of disillusionment, decay and bitterness became widespread. In *Measure for Measure*, said Una Ellis-Fermor, 'the lowest depths of Jacobean negation are touched'.[35] Such an argument could be supported by citation of the more cynical, tortured poems of Donne and the speeches on death, decay and corruption in the drama of Webster, Middleton and Marston. One objection is that 'the cultural climate' was as mixed and variable as the English weather. Against the claim that, around the time of James's accession in 1603, the public mood darkened, can be set the evidence that many people regarded his accession with relief and new-found confidence: after the long decades of concern that the death of the childless Elizabeth might result in conflict about the succession to the throne, the transition was managed efficiently and peacefully.[36] Again, if bitter elements in the 'problem plays' derive from the cultural

44

atmosphere, it is remarkable that within half-a-dozen years Shakespeare is writing *Macbeth* and *Antony and Cleopatra*, which in tone differ markedly from each other and from those four plays. The Jacobean age was the age of Donne's sermons and Jonson's satires, but it was also the age of festive court masques and of Shakespeare's late romances.

Thus, both these explanatory hypotheses are questionable. Nevertheless, Boas's notion of the enigmatic 'problem plays' became influential. In 1910 Ernest Jones offered the Freudian 'Oedipus Complex' as a solution to the enigma of *Hamlet*;[37] and in 1919 T. S. Eliot argued that that play was 'the "Mona Lisa" of literature': 'probably more people have thought *Hamlet* a work of art because they found it interesting, than have found it interesting because it is a work of art'. Indeed, said Eliot, it 'is most certainly an artistic failure'; and he explained this 'failure' by suggesting that Shakespeare was attempting to pour a quart of morbid feelings into the pint pot of the play: the author's feelings flow into Hamlet, but the dramatic context does not supply evidence to justify them: the play lacks 'an objective correlative'.

Hamlet is up against the difficulty that his disgust is occasioned by his mother, but that his mother is not an adequate equivalent for it; his disgust envelops and exceeds her.

Within a few lines, Eliot veers into apparent self-contradiction by stating that there is, after all, a perfectly appropriate disparity between Hamlet's disgust and the Gertrude who is not disgusting:

To have heightened the criminality of Gertrude would have been to provide the formula for a totally different emotion in Hamlet; it is just *because* her character is so negative and insignificant that she arouses in Hamlet the feeling which she is incapable of representing.[38]

Fourteen years later, Eliot remarked that though *Hamlet*, *Troilus and Cressida*, *All's Well That Ends Well* and *Measure for Measure* are 'partial failures', 'if any one of Shakespeare's plays were omitted we should not be able to understand the rest as well as we do':

In such plays, we must consider not only the degree of unification of all the elements into a 'unity of sentiment', but the quality and kind of the emotions to be unified. . . . .[39]

Eliot's idea (partly influenced by Freudian theory), that a literary work may be marred if its author is experiencing emotional confusion or repression and is unable to control or 'objectify' such emotion in the text, became pervasive. F. R. Leavis and the critics associated with Leavis's periodical *Scrutiny* became adept at close textual analyses which purported to reveal a given work's integrity or confusion, though these writers placed somewhat greater emphasis on moral than on emotional coordination – 'sensibility' and 'responsiveness to life' proved to be conveniently capacious terms in the discussions. Given that scrupulous close analysis promised to bring greater objectivity to literary evaluation, it was remarkable that the 'problem plays' occasioned intense disagreement among the *Scrutiny* writers. In 'The Ambiguity of *Measure for Measure*' (*Scrutiny* X, 1942), L. C. Knights supported Hazlitt's claim that in the play 'our sympathies are repulsed and defeated in all directions'. The presentation of Claudio and his offence is 'blurred', said Knights: it 'seems to spring from feelings at war with themselves'; and finally in the play 'the paradox of human law – related on one side to justice and on the other to expediency – is felt as confusion rather than as a sharply focused dilemma'. This essay promptly provoked a stern rejoinder from F. R. Leavis, who, in 'The Greatness of *Measure for Measure*' (also published in *Scrutiny* X) declared that *Measure for Measure* 'seems to me one of the very greatest of the plays, and most consummate and convincing of Shakespeare's achievements'. Praising the view (of G. Wilson Knight in *The Wheel of Fire*) that the play consistently vindicates a New Testament ethic, Leavis argued that Knights had mistaken subtlety for uncertainty and complexity for ambiguity. Only an 'innocent' or immature critic, he suggested, could see the play as cynical or divided.[40]

Meanwhile, Boas's category of 'problem plays' had been energetically adapted by W. W. Lawrence in *Shakespeare's Problem Comedies* (1931). The 'problem comedies' were *Troilus and Cressida, All's Well That Ends Well* and *Measure for Measure*. In them,

a perplexing and distressing complication in human life is presented in a spirit of high seriousness. This special treatment distinguishes such a play from other kinds of drama, in that the theme is handled so as to arouse not merely interest or excitement, or pity or amusement, but to probe the complicated interrelations of character and action, in a situation admitting of different ethical interpretations. The 'problem' is not like one in mathematics, to which there is a single true solution, but is one of conduct, as to which there are no fixed and immutable laws.[41]

Lawrence's detailed discussion of *Measure for Measure*, however, suggested that what made the play problematic was less the presence of a difficult ethical question than the occurrence of a marked generic tension in the basic constitutents of the narrative. Shakespeare was mixing realism with romance; and whereas Shakespeare's original audiences could adapt easily to such a mixture, modern audiences experience the mixture as conflict and become uncertain of their bearings. The main source for *Measure for Measure* was George Whetstone's *Promos and Cassandra*, and in adapting Whetstone's play Shakespeare made two big additions to the story. One was the device of the 'bed-trick' (to preserve Isabella's virginity); the other was the device of the 'ruler in disguise' (to facilitate the bed-trick). But both these devices are ancient and traditional: they belong to the world of legend and folk-tale, whereas other parts of the play are modern and innovatory, psychologically complex and realistically plausible. The basic situation, Isabella's choice between death for Claudio or dishonour for herself, is presented with considerable realism, but

this realistic basic action is combined with plot-material taken from traditional story, and exhibiting the archaisms and improbabilities characteristic of such narrative. The introduction of these artificial elements was chiefly due to Shakespeare, not to his sources. This point seems generally to have been overlooked. The extraordinary thing is that while the main situation apparently stirred Shakespeare very deeply, and while he gave to it a power such as no other writer had attained, he made it in some respects more conventional, less like real life. The result has been confusion among the commentators. They have been puzzled by the contradictions arising from the fusion of realism and artificiality, and they have failed to understand the significance of the changes made by Shakespeare. 'What is wrong with this play?' asks Quiller-Couch. 'Evidently *something* is wrong, since the critics so tangle themselves in apologies and interpretations.'[42]

Commentators have seen Isabella both as saintly and as 'something rancid in her chastity',[43] Mariana as poignant and as immoral, the Duke as nobly wise and as a cynical schemer. The whole confusion stems from the modern failure to see that while Shakespeare is partly a realist, he has co-ordinated the plot by drawing on 'story-book business – Haroun al Raschid disguised, Substituted Bride, Severed Head, and the various mechanical tricks and turnings of a complicated *dénouement*'.[44] The problems dwindle if we simply let our imagination be as promiscuous as Shakespeare's and adopt extremely flexible criteria, accepting some parts as realistic and others as 'romantic' and archaic, while remembering that what seems offensive to modern audiences would have seemed familiar and acceptable to Shakespeare's.

Such flexibility seemed to be plain inconsistency to E. M. W. Tillyard. In *Shakespeare's Problem Plays* (1950), Tillyard adopted the grouping established by Boas in 1896 (*Hamlet, Troilus and Cressida, All's Well That Ends Well* and *Measure for Measure*) but opened his book with the disarming claim that he intended to use the term 'problem plays' 'vaguely and equivocally, as a matter of convenience'. He divided the group into two, thus: '*Hamlet* and *Troilus and Cressida* are problem plays because they deal with and display interesting problems; *All's Well* and *Measure for Measure* because they *are* problems': the latter two 'have something radically schizophrenic about them'.[45] Tillyard's case for the 'schizophrenic' nature of *Measure for Measure* derives partly from Lawrence, whom he frequently cites; but he argues that modern dissatisfaction with the play stems from no anachronistic demand for consistent realism but rather from recognition that the play criticizes itself by exposing the plot's betrayal of its own best endeavours.

[I]n *Measure for Measure* realism admits no folk-lore for half of the play, while all the folk-lore occurs in the second half . . . . . In *All's Well* we have been habituated to the improbable, the conventional, and the antique: in *Measure for Measure* the change to these from the more lifelike human passions is too violent; and it is here a case not of a modern prudery unaware of Elizabethan preconceptions but of an artistic breach of internal harmony.[46]

The difference is one in quality, not merely in convention. The changes in the plot, which had been introduced to preserve Isabella's chastity, made it impossible for Shakespeare 'to carry the play through in the spirit in which he began it'. As the Duke emerges as the central manipulator, the quality of the characterization declines: Isabella, for example, loses her independence and becomes subservient. Above all, there is a marked decline in the poetic richness of the play.

Up to III.i.151, when the Duke enters to interrupt the passionate conversation between Claudio and Isabella on the conflicting claims of his life and her chastity, the play is predominantly poetical, the poetry being, it is true, set off by passages of animated prose. And the poetry is of that kind of which Shakespeare is the great master, the kind that seems extremely close to the business of living, the problem of how to function as a human being . . . . . From the Duke's entry at III.i.151 to the end of the play there is little poetry of any kind and scarcely any of the kind described above.[47]

Thus, by using a Leavisite criterion, that of textural vitality, Tillyard was led to a general judgement of the play which flatly contradicted that of F. R. Leavis.

The books by Boas, Lawrence and Tillyard were at least congruent in their choice of texts, so that a reader who subsequently heard the term 'Shakespeare's problem plays' could be reasonably certain that the plays in question were *Troilus and Cressida*, *All's Well That Ends Well* and *Measure for Measure*, and probably *Hamlet* too. Such reasonable certainty was then dispelled in 1963 by the appearance of Ernest Schanzer's *The Problem Plays of Shakespeare*. Schanzer claimed that the eligible plays were just three in number, and those not the predictable trio. Yes, *Measure for Measure* was there, as usual; but the other two were now *Julius Caesar* and *Antony and Cleopatra*. He defined the 'problem play' thus:

A play in which we find a concern with a moral problem which is central to it, presented in such a manner that we are unsure of our moral bearings, so that uncertain and divided responses to it in the minds of the audience are possible or even probable.[48]

In such works, Shakespeare practises 'dramatic coquetry' in his presentation of the main characters, 'playing fast and loose with our affections for them, engaging and alienating them in turn'.[49]

Schanzer excludes *All's Well That Ends Well* from the 'problem plays' on the grounds that the original audience would have accepted as unproblematic Helena's stratagems to get into bed with her disdainful husband; nor would *Troilus and Cressida* have seemed problematic, he states, for the return of Helen to Menelaus is obviously the correct moral course, even if the Trojans do not follow it; and nor would *Hamlet*, for though Hamlet's psychology may be complex it reveals no 'central moral problem' – the ethics of revenge are not questioned. *Julius Caesar* is admitted to the category because the central question, 'the conflicting claims of the realm of personal relations and that of politics', is presented in a way which divides us: our sympathies go now to Caesar and now against him, now to the conspirators and now against them. In *Antony and Cleopatra* the central problem is that of deciding whether the love of Antony and Cleopatra is noble or base, and the technique of 'dramatic coquetry' is used to the utmost: 'As regards the two lovers, it is employed from the very beginning until the fourth act. As for Caesar, it extends through the entire play up to its closing lines'. Schanzer claims that *Measure for Measure* conforms to his definition because it has a central moral problem, the question of whether Isabella was right to decline to sacrifice her virginity to save Claudio, and this is presented in such a way (by means of 'dramatic coquetry' in the treatment of Isabella's character) as to make us uncertain of our moral bearings.[50]

Some obvious objections could be made both to Schanzer's case about *Measure for Measure* and to his claim that the 'problem plays' are just three in number. Our attitude to Isabella's choice may be divided, but if this is a problem for us, it is only one of a cluster of problems, and others in that cluster may be much bigger: for example, what exactly, in a Christian state, should be the right balance between mercy and justice? Is 'a Christian state' a contradiction in terms? How should we finally judge the Duke? What is the correct course between sexual puritanism and sexual licence? Why are there apparent contradictions in the sexual politics of the play? And why are there marked discrepancies between a textural scansion (in which we give priority to scanning the texture of the verse and characterization) and a moral-thematic scansion (in which we give priority to scanning the more paraphrasable thematic development)?

Again, Schanzer's isolation of just three plays seems strange. If indeed a 'problem play' is one that presents a central moral issue in ways that divide us, and in which 'dramatic coquetry' is prominent, then many of Shakespeare's plays – probably most of them – could fall into this category. Shakespeare has long been famed for the complexity of his presentation of life. If *Julius Caesar* is a 'problem play', so must be *Richard II*, in which our judgement of Richard, Bolingbroke, and the deposition and killing of the monarch is made particularly problematic by Shakespeare's treatment (now searching, now reticent) of the source-material; so, therefore, must be *1* and *2 Henry IV*; and so must even be *Henry V*, which dramatizes a tension between Christian and martial kingship and shows a Henry who sometimes seeks to transfer to others his burden of moral responsibility. Schanzer could have included *King Lear*, with its notoriously troubling dramatization of the problem of theodicy; or *Othello*, which has radically divided major commentators, some seeing Othello as noble victim, others seeing him as egoistic self-deceiver. At any time, a brilliant new production or a craftily egregious essay may problematize a text previously regarded as unproblematic.

Schanzer endeavoured to give new rigour and precision to the definition of the 'problem play', but his definition was far more elastically capacious than he seems to have recognized; and, by offering an unorthodox trio of plays, he marred the referential convenience of the term. Anyone who now refers to 'The problem plays of Shakespeare' will need to specify and justify the particular selection of texts that he or she has in mind. Schanzer's concern has been overtaken by a widespread and protean movement which largely characterizes literary criticism in the latter half of the twentieth century. In this period, whether the critic purports to be traditionalist, structuralist, post-structuralist, deconstructionist, Marxist, semiotician or psychoanalytic in approach, or a combination of some of these, it is likely that his or her work will place heavy emphasis on the value of perceiving states of radical paradox or contradiction in the texts under discussion. Partly, this has been a reaction against the previous critical over-emphasis on the value of seeing a good literary text as 'an organic whole'. Partly, it is an expression of increasing political scepticism about established authorities, communities and hierarchies. In critical writings, the 'binarist fallacy' has become widespread: complexities are reduced to binary oppositions, tension is magnified as conflict, and a qualified meaning is melodramatized as a subverted meaning. J. W. Lever remarks: 'Twentieth-century taste, in art as in life, welcomes the discordant and the extreme, but is insensitive to the virtues of the mean: understandably, most modern critics have been preoccupied with the tensions in the earlier part of the play, and have projected upon Shakespeare an unlikely degree of sanctity or cynicism.'[51] ('Without Contraries is no progression', said William Blake.) What Lever's own analysis suggests, however, is that if Shakespeare gave his ethical assent to 'the mean', he gave his imaginative energy to the conflict of extremes.

The dramatic poetry of the first half of the play, with its free-ranging, esemplastic imagery and flexible speech-rhythms, gave way to a sententious prose, stiff gnomic couplets, and a blank verse which, though generally dignified, was basically uninspired. The Duke's Apollonian intellect resolved all conflicts in society and stilled all tumults in the soul; but in the process the autonomy of the individual was lost, and with it his innate right to choose as between evil and good. At the same time the Duke himself, a prisoner of his own exemplary image, failed as an authentic human being and remained a stage device, midway between personality and type.[52]

In sonnet 66, Shakespeare says:

> *Tir'd with all these, for restful death I cry:*
> *As, to behold desert a beggar born,*
> *And needy nothing trimm'd in jollity . . . . .*
> *And strength by limping sway disablèd,*
> *And art made tongue-tied by authority . . . . .*

'And art made tongue-tied by authority': perhaps these words epitomize one of the most disturbing features of *Measure for Measure*. If we are sensitive to the textures of the poetry and the vitalities of the characterization, we will notice that they do become relatively muted, if not 'tongue-tied', as the Duke resumes full power towards the play's close. The Duke's authority may command Shakespeare's intellectual or ethical assent, yet still elicit his ontological or imaginative dissent. Shakespeare had always sensed some contradiction between strong political *order* and ontological *vitality* – richness, fullness or vividness of being. In *2 Henry IV*, the price immediately paid for the emergence of Henry V as upright monarch is the chilly dismissal of the exuberant Falstaff. Later, in *Antony and Cleopatra*, the astute Octavius will prevail, while Antony, with all his gusto for life, will fall; and the chaste Octavia will be ethically superior, but pallid compared with the riggish Cleopatra with 'her infinite variety'. Shakespeare's plays demonstrate in numerous ways – even in their very verse-movements and metaphoric textures – his experience of the tension between the claims of rational order and the claims of rich exuberance.

He valued the social restraints on the 'universal wolf' of appetitive egotism; yet he knew that each of us may harbour a voracious sense of possessing more life than ordered social existence permits us to express.

2.5   Source-Materials

Possible source-materials for *Measure for Measure* may be identified and classified in various ways. The influence of relatively private and personal experience has been considered in sections 2.1 and 2.3; while that of topical news and debates of the day has been indicated in section 2.21. In this section, I consider a selection of possible biblical, historical, legendary and literary sources. Some of the items are generally acknowledged to have had a direct influence on the play, but others have a more controversial status.

   The adducing of published source-materials has a variety of uses. First, we learn something about cultural history and the traditions within which a text can be located. Secondly, we may learn about the creative process; and by perceiving how a writer has adapted his source-materials, we may gain a clearer idea of his imaginative intentions. Thirdly, we may hope thereby to resolve some critical problems and establish a more authoritative judgement of the text. Since one cannot, in logic, deduce a value judgement from a statement of fact, it is the third of these uses which is the most debatable. One difficulty was indicated in section 2.4 by the difference between W. W. Lawrence's conclusions and E. M. W. Tillyard's. Lawrence said that modern audiences may sense a conflict between the relatively realistic and relatively non-realistic aspects of the play. Consideration of the main literary sources showed that Shakespeare had deliberately departed from those sources by increasing the quantity of traditional, folk-tale material. As such material was evidently to the taste of Shakespeare and his audiences, we should respect their flexibility of response, see in perspective the modern predilection for the realistic, and thereby increase our appreciation and enjoyment of the play. Tillyard, however, while accepting that Shakespeare had deliberately added to the 'archaic' or 'folk-tale' elements of the work, claimed that this did not vindicate them. We should be guided by the texture of the poetry and the vitality of the characterization, he said, and we would then be led to the conclusion that these 'archaic' elements had marred the quality of the work.

To those who say that what matters is the result, the text as we have it, and not the source-materials, one answer is that a comparison with sources can define the distinctive and valuable features of the text. The originality that counts in a work of literature is not necessarily a matter of independence from prior literary materials but rather a matter of the quality of articulate experience. This should be borne in mind during the following survey.

2.51 *Biblical*

(i) The Doctrine of the Atonement

The Atonement is the reconciliation of man with God by means of the incarnation and death of Jesus Christ. The eating of the forbidden fruit by Adam and Eve had been an act of disobedience which had estranged God from man and had consigned all people to death. After many centuries, God, in the form of Jesus Christ, entered the world to live as man and be crucified, thus becoming 'a sacrifice, not only for original guilt, but also for all actual sins of men'. This death reconciled man to God and gave all people the possibility that they might gain eternal life. Such is the doctrine.

'I perceive your Grace, like power divine,/Hath looked upon my passes', says Angelo to the Duke in *Measure for Measure* (V.i.367–8). G. Wilson Knight claimed that the Duke resembles Jesus and that his ethic is really that of the Gospel.[53] Roy Battenhouse, following Wilson Knight, argued that the play should be seen as an allegory of the Atonement. The Duke, like Jesus, comes to teach and judge mankind: he 'works as a sort of secret, omniscient, and omnipresent Providence'.[54] His very title, Duke, means 'leader', and the name 'Vincentio' means 'victor or conqueror', while 'Isabella' means 'devoted to God'. As for the Duke's proposal of marriage to Isabella, this too can be seen, with Pauline warrant, as part of the allegory of the Atonement:

Wiues, submit your selues vnto your housbands, as vnto the Lord.

For the housband is the wiues head, euen as Christ is the head of the Church, & the same is the sauiour of his bodie.

Therefore as the Church is in subiection to Christ, euen so the wiues be to their housbands in euerie thing.

Housbands, loue your wiues, euen as Christ loued the Church, & gaue him self for it . . . . .

For this cause shal a man leaue father & mother, & shal cleaue to his wife, & they twaine shalbe one flesh.

This is a great secret, but I speake concerning Christ, & concerning the Church.

(Geneva Bible: St Paul: Ephesians V: 22–5, 31–2)

The view that *Measure for Measure* is largely a dramatization of the Christian Atonement was supported by Nevill Coghill[55] and influenced various productions of the play in the 1950s. I think that recollections of the doctrine of the Atonement were a significant though not dominant source for Shakespeare, and they are given movingly dramatic expression by Isabella in Act I I, scene ii:

ANGELO   *Your brother is a forfeit of the law,*
            And you but waste your words.

ISABELLA   *Alas, alas!*
            Why, all the souls that were, were forfeit once,
            And He that might the vantage best have took
            Found out the remedy.

The 'remedy' was the Incarnation; and the sense that there is a hierarchy of judgement and mercy extending beyond this earth is an important part of the drama's ethical discussion. Occasionally the tone of the play does modulate strongly towards the allegorical, as in the Duke's gnomic speech beginning 'He who the sword of heaven will bear' (III.ii.254ff.). The dramatic complexities and particularly the fallibilities in the Duke's character may cause the reader to doubt, however, that references to the Atonement are as dominant or as consistent as Battenhouse claimed.

(ii) The Sermon on the Mount

According to St Luke's Gospel, V I: 36–42, Jesus said:

Be ye therefore merciful, as your Father also is merciful.

Iudge not, and ye shal not be iudged: condemne not, and ye shal not be condemned: forgiue, and ye shalbe forgiuen.

Giue, and it shalbe giuen vnto you: a good measure, pressed downe, shaken together and running ouer shal men giue into your bosome: for with what measure ye mette, with the same shal men mette to you againe.

And he spake a parable vnto them, Can the blinde lead the blinde? shal they not bothe fall into the ditch?

The disciple is not aboue his master: but whosoeuer wil be a perfect disciple, shal be as his master.

And why seest thou a mote in thy brothers eye, and considerest not the beame, that is in thine owne eye?

54

Ether how canst thou saye to thy brother, Brother, let me pul out
is in thine eye, when thou seest not the beame that is in thine owne ey
cast out the beame out of thine owne eye first, & then shalt thou se pe
out the mote that is in thy brothers eye.[56]

J. M. Nosworthy comments:

The relevance of this to the whole fabric of *Measure for Measure*, even down to
the play's title, is self-evident. The Sermon on the Mount is, in effect, one of
Shakespeare's main sources, and he uses it, together with other passages from the
Gospels, to enrich and illuminate moral attitudes which were already present in
[George Whetstone's] *Promos and Cassandra* but which, judging from the frequency
with which they are invoked in other plays, were substantially those to which he
himself subscribed.[57]

Those 'moral attitudes' include the belief that mercy must season justice,
memorably expressed by Portia's 'quality of mercy' speech in *The Merchant of Venice*, IV.i.179–97, as well as by Isabella in *Measure for Measure*,
II.ii.49–142; and the related belief that we should do as we would be done
by, which had been expressed by, among others, Lord Say in *2 Henry VI*,
IV.vii, and the Lord Chief Justice in *2 Henry IV*, V.ii.

(iii) On Fornication and Adultery

In the Old Testament, the Mosaic Law had said:

And if a man entise a mayd that is not betrothed, & lye with her, he shal endowe
her, and take her to his wife.
If her father refuse to giue her to him, he shal pay money, according to the dowrie
of virgines.

(Exodus XXII: 16–17)

And the man that committeth adulterie with another mans wife, because he
hathe committed adulterie with his neighbours wife, the adulterer and the adulteress
shal dye the death.

(Leviticus XX: 10)

In the New Testament, however, Jesus waives the death-sentence for
adultery:

Then the Scribes, & the Pharises broght vnto him a woman, taken in adulterie,
& set her in the middes,
And said vnto him, Master, this woman was taken in adulterie, in the verie act.
Now Moses in the Law commanded vs, that suche shulde be stoned: what saist
thou therefore?
And this they said to tempt him, that thei might haue, wherof to accuse him. But
Iesus stouped downe, and with his finger wrote on the grounde.

And while they continued asking him, he lift him self vp, & said vnto them, Let him that is among you without sinne, cast the first stone at her.

And againe he stouped downe, and wrote on the grounde.

And when they heard it, being accused by their owne conscience, they went out one by one, beginning at the eldest euen to the last: so Iesus was left alone, and the woman standing in the middes.

When Iesus had lift vp him self againe, and sawe no man, but the woman, he said vnto her, Woman, where are those thine accusers? hathe no man condemned thee?

She said, No man, Lord. And Iesus said, Nether do I condemne thee: go and sinne no more.

(John VIII: 3–11)

As narrative, this passage is memorably realistic ('And againe he stouped downe, and wrote on the grounde'; 'they went out one by one, beginning at the eldest'). As morality, it is one of the glories of Christianity. This sacred instance of forgiveness instead of punishment for sexual sin may readily be brought to mind by the situations of *Measure for Measure*, and the memory may transmit authority to the Duke's eventual lenience to Claudio, Juliet, and particularly to Angelo. J. M. Nosworthy claims, however, that Jesus's attitude to the woman taken in adultery does emphasize by contrast the fact that Isabella partly shares the distorted values of Angelo. At II.iv.42–9, Angelo actually declares that it would be as ethical to pardon a murderer as to pardon two lovers who have copulated and procreated outside holy wedlock. At II.ii.29–31, Isabella says:

> There is a vice that most I do abhor,
> And most desire should meet the blow of justice;
> For which I would not plead, but that I must . . . . .

Nosworthy comments:

If Claudio's slip (or, indeed, premarital intercourse in any degree) is the vice that she most abhors, she must surely stand convicted of a gross ineptitude in moral judgement. The Church's teaching on illicit sexual intercourse is unequivocal, but it is questionable whether any creed in any age has regarded this as the most abhorrent of all sins.[58]

2.52 *Historical:* Basilikon Doron

Before gaining the English throne, James VI of Scotland wrote *Basilikon Doron*, a manual of statesmanship for his son and heir. The first edition, of just seven copies, was printed in Edinburgh in 1599; and in 1603, the year in which he transferred his court to London, a further edition appeared in Edinburgh and two editions were published in London. Some scholars believe that Shakespeare read this work and that it had a direct influence on the content of *Measure for Measure*; others believe that any resemblances between the book and the play are coincidental, given that both repeat a number of traditional commonplaces of statecraft. Even if it is not a direct source, *Basilikon Doron* still illuminates the play.

James advises his son to be a model of pious virtue: 'as your company should be a paterne to the rest of the people, so should your person be a lampe and mirour to your company: giuing light to your seruants to walke in the path of vertue . . . . .'[59] Of the four cardinal virtues, 'make one of them, which is Temperance, Queene of all the rest within you'.[60]

Vse Iustice, but with such moderation, as it turne not in Tyrannie . . . . . for lawes are ordained as rules of vertuous and sociall liuing, and not to bee snares to trap your good subjects: and therefore the lawe must be interpreted according to the meaning, and not to the literall sense thereof . . . . .

And aboue all, let the measure of your loue to euery one, be according to the measure of his vertue . . . . . [61]

The Prince should 'hate no man more than a proude Puritane', partly because Puritans are inclined 'to fantasie to themselues a Democraticke forme of gouernment'.[62] He should particularly beware of slanderers who 'iudge and speake rashly of their Prince, setting the Common-weale vpon foure props, as wee call it; euer wearying of the present estate, and desirous of nouelties'.[63] (Compare the Duke's 'Novelty is only in request . . . . . There is scarce truth enough alive to make societies secure': III.ii.217–18, 220–21.) When sitting in judgement, the Prince should beware of intermediaries:

suffer no Aduocates to be heard there with their dilatours, but let euery partie tell his owne tale himselfe: and wearie not to heare the complaints of the oppressed . . . . . [64]

If much of this advice seems predictable and perhaps commonplace, there are still some features of *Basilikon Doron* which are less predictable and can clearly be related to *Measure for Measure*. They strengthen, though they do not confirm, the claim that Shakespeare had direct knowledge of King James's work. James says that the Prince has a duty to seek a pure and virtuous wife, and should keep his own body 'cleane and vnpolluted, till yee giue it to your wife, whom-to onely it belongeth':

For how can ye iustly craue to bee ioyned with a pure virgine, if your bodie be polluted? why should the one halfe bee cleane, and the other defiled? And although I know, fornication is thought but a light and a veniall sinne, by the most part of the world, yet remember well what I said to you in my first Booke anent conscience, and count euery sinne and breach of Gods law, not according as the vaine world esteemeth of it, but as God the Iudge and maker of the lawe accounteth of the same. Heare God commanding by the mouth of *Paul*, to *abstaine from fornication*, declaring that the *fornicator shall not inherite the Kingdome of heauen* . . . . . [65]

When discussing justice, James says that a tyrant 'would enter like a Saint while he found himselfe fast vnder-foot, and then would suffer his vnrulie affections to burst foorth'; whereas the true king, on inheriting power, should first implement the law with full severity, and only subsequently show mercy:

And when yee haue by the seueritie of Iustice once setled your countries, and made them know that ye can strike, then may ye thereafter all the daies of your life mixe Iustice with Mercie, punishing or sparing, as ye shall finde the crime to haue been wilfully or rashly committed, and according to the by-past behauiour of the committer. [66]

James then proceeds to make what is, for our purposes, the remarkably relevant admission that when he first came to the Scottish throne, he had done the opposite of what he is now commending: he had been too clement, so that the law fell into disrespect and disorder flourished.

For if otherwise ye kyth your clemencie at the first, the offences would soone come to such heapes, and the contempt of you grow so great, that when ye would fall to punish, the number of them to be punished, would exceed the innocent; and yee would be troubled to resolue whom-at to begin: and against your nature would be compelled then to wracke many, whom the chastisement of few in the beginning might haue preserued. But in this, my ouerdeare bought experience may serue you for a sufficient lesson: For I confesse, where I thought (by being gracious at the beginning) to win all mens hearts to a louing and willing obedience, I by the contrary found, the disorder of the countrie, and the losse of my thankes to be all my reward. [67]

This passage can readily be related to *Measure for Measure*, I.iii.19–39, in which the Duke explains that he had erred in lenience; to the Friar-Duke's complaint (V.i.314–19) that the laws have stood 'as much in mock as mark'; and to Angelo's defence of awakened justice (II.ii.91–105).

2.53 *Legendary and Fictional*

(i) The Motif of the Disguised Ruler

In *Measure for Measure*, the Duke is thought to have travelled far from his people, but he remains in disguise as an observer and instructor before revealing himself and reasserting his authority. The basis of such a plot is an archetypal narrative pattern. An archetypal pattern is one which is ancient, simple, and susceptible to myriad subsequent adaptations: it can be elaborated as narrative and fleshed conceptually in numerous ways, whether as myth, legend, folk-tale or realistic fiction. So there are many precedents and analogues, remote or near, for the 'disguised ruler' of the play.

One remote and exalted analogue is, of course, biblical. God Himself, ruler of mankind, had moved among His people as Jesus of Nazareth, a carpenter's son; and in the days after the Crucifixion when His disciples feared that He was dead, He was still walking among them unrecognized, as on the journey to Emmaus (Luke XXIV: 13–53). In classical legend, one of the most famous disguised rulers is Odysseus, who, at the end of *The Odyssey*, returns to his homestead in the guise of a poor vagabond, assesses the loyalties of his family and servants, and eventually reveals himself and wreaks ruthless vengeance on his wife's suitors and their helpers. A mixture of classical and medieval is the fourteenth-century poem *Sir Orfeo*, in which Orfeo, descendant of Juno and King of Winchester, returns from ordeals in the guise of a beggar-minstrel and tests the loyalty of his steward before identifying himself and resuming his rule.

In the sixteenth century, English social reformers praised the historic example set by the Roman emperor, Alexander Severus (who ruled from 222 to 235 A.D.). In his endeavours to stamp out vice and corruption, Severus was reputed to have walked through Rome in various disguises (now as scholar, now as merchant) and to have staged a public trial at which various malicious witnesses against one Geminus were confronted and exposed by counter-witnesses. George Whetstone's *A Mirrour for Magistrates of Cyties* (1584) said that the methods of Severus were now needed to check the growth of vice in London.[68] One echo in *Measure for Measure* of the accounts of Severus is the name of one of the Duke's friends, Varrius: for Severus's father was named Varius. In literary works of the late sixteenth and early seventeenth centuries, disguised potentates made frequent appearances: for example, in Barnabe Riche's romance *The Adventures of Brusanus Prince of Hungarie*, and in the anonymous plays *A Knack to Know a Knave, Sir John Oldcastle* and *George a Greene*. Other examples are Felice and Malevole in Marston's *Antonio and Mellida* and *The Malcontent*. On the eve of the battle of Agincourt, Shakespeare's Henry V wanders among his troops in the guise of a common soldier and is obliged to defend the royal conduct of war when he hears the shrewd criticisms by Bates and particularly by Williams. J. W. Lever remarks that at its most serious, the legend of the disguised ruler 'confirmed the central humanist concept of royal authority, according to which the true ruler set an example of wisdom, temperance and magnanimity'.[69] The principle of gaining knowledge of others (and thus power over them) through the deception of disguise is, however, one which may produce morally ambiguous situations. A useful distinction is sometimes that between 'Black Machiavellism', in which a variety of deceptions is used for the sake of selfish advancement, and 'White Machiavellism', in which a variety of deceptions is used for the general good. In each case the end is deemed to justify the means, but the ends differ greatly. In the good ruler, the expedient of disguise is usually entailed by distrust of intermediaries or of deputies who have been allocated the task of identifying and redressing injustices; more generally, it serves the end of guarding from subversion the established order.

(ii) The Motif of the Corrupt Magistrate and the Sexual Ransom

In the sixteenth century there circulated numerous versions (often purportedly historical) of the following tale. A man was sentenced to death for murder. While he was awaiting death, his wife appealed to a magistrate for his life to be spared. The magistrate said that if she secretly copulated with him, he would indeed spare her husband. She reluctantly acquiesced, but the magistrate treacherously broke his promise and the execution was effected. The widow then appealed for justice to the ruler of the land; and, as a result of the ensuing investigation, the magistrate was compelled to marry her so as to restore her honour, after which he was promptly executed.

Some of the main elements of this story have been traced to the writings of St Augustine of Hippo (354–430). The relevant passage can conveniently be found in Geoffrey Bullough's *Narrative and Dramatic Sources of Shakespeare*, II, 418–19: it concerns a woman who, with her husband's consent, sleeps with a rich man in the hope of saving the husband from death. The sixteenth-century versions include those of Claude Rouillet in his tragedy *Philanira* (1556) and of Giambattista Giraldi – better known as Giraldi Cinthio – in both *Hecatommithi* (1565) and *Epitia* (written *circa* 1570), as well as George Whetstone's *Promos and Cassandra* (1578), Thomas Lupton's *Too Good To Be True* (1581) and de Belleforest's *Histoires Tragiques* (1582). Of these, the versions by Lupton, Cinthio and Whetstone are known to have provided material for Shakespeare's play. Shakespeare follows Lupton in using a basic time-scheme of a few days and in presenting lengthy ethical arguments between the interceding woman and the magistrate. Cinthio changed the story significantly by letting the original offence of the doomed man be rape rather than murder and by letting the pleader be his sister rather than a wife. Furthermore the heroine (Epitia) copulates with the magistrate only after obtaining from him a promise of marriage – albeit one which he does not intend to keep. These changes permitted a less draconian dénouement. In Cinthio's tale, the Emperor who hears the accusations made against a governor (Iuriste or Juriste) by the deflowered young woman decrees that the corrupt man must marry her and then be executed; yet, shortly after her marriage to Juriste, the woman (Epitia) appeals again to the Emperor:

'But just as, before I was his wife, I had to desire your Majesty to condemn him to the death which you have most justly assigned him, so now, when according to your pleasure I am bound to Juriste in the sacred bonds of matrimony, I should, if I consented to his death, regard myself as deserving perpetual infamy as a pitiless and cruel woman ..... Your Majesty's sentence has given clear proof of your Justice; now may it please you, as I sincerely beg, to manifest your Clemency by giving him to me alive.

'It is, most sacred Majesty, no less praise for him who holds the government of the world as now your Majesty most worthily holds it, to exercise Clemency as to show Justice. For whereas Justice shows that Vices are hateful and punishes them accordingly, Clemency makes a monarch most like to the immortal Gods.'[70]

The Emperor does indeed grant clemency, and Epitia lives happily ever after with Juriste.

When converting his tale into the play *Epitia*, Cinthio made further mitigations of the grimmer elements of the plot. After the Emperor has pronounced his twofold sentence, both Juriste's sister and Epitia's aunt fail to persuade her to plead for Juriste's life; but then it is discovered that Epitia's brother, Vico, has not been executed. Pitying the doomed youth, an officer has secretly kept him alive, substituting the head of an executed criminal for that of Vico. Epitia now begs the Emperor to pardon Vico, which he does, 'since the girl he raped forgives him and he is willing to marry her'; and next she seeks pardon for Juriste, 'now the cruel cause is moved/For which he was condemned':[71] and this, too, the Emperor grants. In the last scene of *Epitia*, the Captain of Justice remarks: 'Vico is saved, Iuriste is saved, Epitia's honour is saved, and so too is the honour of the woman violated by Vico': succinctness anticipating that of the Duke

61

in *Measure for Measure*, III.i.253–6: 'by this is your brother saved, your honour untainted, the poor Mariana advantaged, and the corrupt deputy scaled'.[72] Thus, some of Cinthio's innovations bring the plot closer to that of Shakespeare's subsequent play; and, in the characterization of Epitia, her eloquence and her declaration that her honour is dearer to her than is the life of her brother anticipate those features in Isabella. The whole of *Epitia* has a strenuously ethical tone. It will be noted, however, that the original offence of Vico remains rape (not forbidden copulation with his betrothed), that Epitia is no novitiate but a vigorously worldly heroine, and that Epitia's plea for Juriste is made not only after her marriage to him but also after she has discovered that her brother is alive.

Without doubt, the major literary source of *Measure for Measure* is George Whetstone's play, *Promos and Cassandra*. Its plot follows this course. In the city of Julio, Lord Promos has received from the distant King of Hungary a commission to maintain justice and extirpate abuses. Young Andrugio is arrested and sentenced to death for fornication with his fiancée, Polina. At his request, his sister, Cassandra, approaches Promos and begs that the death-sentence be commuted. She emphasizes that the law was made to punish lechers, not lovers who intend marriage. Promos is sexually attracted to Cassandra, and, after inner turmoil, tells her that only if she copulates with him will he deliver Andrugio from jail: 'my wife I may thee make', he adds. Cassandra consults her imprisoned brother. Although she thinks that death is better than dishonour, Andrugio argues that an enforced evil is no evil: 'For in forst faultes is no intent of yll'.[73] She therefore submits to Promos' lust, but he abides by the letter rather than the spirit of his promise to deliver Andrugio from jail: he commands the jailer to proceed with the execution and send the dead man's head to Cassandra. She then decides to appeal for justice to the King of Hungary, who has her claims investigated and, on his ceremonial entry to the city, confronts Promos with the accusations. Promos quickly admits his guilt. The King decrees that Promos must marry Cassandra to restore her honour, and then be executed. After the marriage, Cassandra is moved by a sense of wifely duty and by pity for Promos' plight to beg for his life. Her pleas seem to be in vain, and Promos is led away to the scaffold. Unknown to Cassandra, her brother lives. The jailer had taken pity on him, had substituted another man's head for his, and had released Andrugio to live in the wilds. Andrugio, learning of Promos' downfall, returns to the city. If he reveals himself, he may (he fears) be re-arrested and executed; but the thought of his sister's grief at the impending fate of Promos eventually overcomes his apprehensions, and he reveals himself to the King. General rejoicing ensues. The King spares Promos, who is reunited with his joyful wife and restored to office; while Andrugio is pardoned on condition that he proceed with his marriage to Polina. 'Justice joyne with mercie evermore', concludes the King.[74]

Thus, Whetstone's plot differs from Cinthio's in various important ways. The original offence is not rape but simply the copulation of lovers in anticipation of marriage. Cassandra's eventual plea for Promos is made before she is aware that her brother has survived. Furthermore, Whetstone likes to display at length states of inner division: Promos' hesitations before presenting his ultimatum to Cassandra, Cassandra's own reluctance to submit (and her subsequent dilemma of choice between shameful life and suicide), and her brother's uncertainty about revealing himself or remaining safe in secret. In these plot-developments and in the dramatization of inner division, Shakespeare has largely, though not entirely, followed Whetstone's adaptation of the material. One big modification appears in the treatment of the ruler. Whetstone's King of Hungary makes a late entry into the action. It is quite a powerful, authoritative entry, for he has much to say on the nature of justice and the need for social equity; but he emerges rather as a *deus ex machina*. Shakespeare's Duke, on the other hand, is constantly present during the unfolding of the action, as observer and as manipulator. This gives greater economy and co-ordination to the plotting; it is he who arranges for the sentenced young man to be saved from execution, and this event no longer depends on the independent and rather fortuitous decision of a merciful jailer. (In its principle of economical co-ordination, this process has a resemblance to Shakespeare's adaptation into *Othello* of Cinthio's tale of Disdemona and the Moor. Shakespeare's Iago is much more intelligent, ingenious and ubiquitous than his counterpart – the wicked Ensign – in the source-tale; and this change not only deepened that characterization but also gave new tautness and compression to the plotting.)

One obvious respect in which Whetstone's *Promos and Cassandra* differs from previous fictional treatments of the 'corrupt magistrate' legend is that Whetstone has been concerned to dramatize extensively the intrigues and corruptions of a whole society. Whetstone offers a full and diverse social panorama, and likes to show how the corruptions of the high are linked to, or paralleled by, those of the low. Thus Promos' coercion of Cassandra is first prompted by the hints of his corrupt official, Phallax, a barrator. In return for sexual favours, Phallax frees an arrested prostitute, Lamia, whose pimp plays a prominent role. Phallax's schemes of extortion are assisted by two rapacious informers, appropriately named Gripax and Rapax. The huge cast also includes a hangman, seen gloating over his perquisites (the suits of his victims), and various penitent prisoners languishing in jail. In scenes of low comedy and knockabout farce, one Grimball is robbed by Rowke and Rosko (the pimp) while being barbered in preparation for a visit to Rosko's mistress. Carpenters, councillors, aldermen, poor citizens, a clown – these and others help to make the play a remarkably full cross-section of sixteenth-century society; and the complicated plotting and sub-plotting serve to illustrate the themes of interactive corruption and the connections between lust, financial greed and injustice. The play was first printed in 1578, so it had been written about a decade before Marlowe and Shakespeare brought their exuberant eloquence to dramatic verse; and it is true that *Promos and Cassandra* sometimes seems ploddingly sententious in its moral ideas and clumpingly naive in its verse. Yet there is formal variety: blank verse, various songs, rhyming hexameters and fourteeners, and a medley of other forms. The dialogue is at its liveliest when Whetstone uses pithily colloquial idioms, as when Phallax describes the swelling desire of Promos for Cassandra:

> *'Tis more than straunge to see Lord* Promos' *plight*
> *He fryskes about as byrdes were in his breech.*
> *Even now he seemes (through hope) to taste delight,*
> *And straight (through feare) where he clawes it doth not ytch.*
> (Part 1, III.v.1–4)

So, although the verse is frequently of the kind (verging on rhymed doggerel) which Shakespeare was to parody in Act V of *A Midsummer Night's Dream*, Whetstone's play has a quality of native, English, homely vitality. It remains a very informative social document (the details of the preparations for the King's arrival say much about Elizabethan festivities); and, by the standards of the 1570s, it is an ambitious play in its scale, social range and variety of thematic development. The play has never been performed in recent times, and its only readers tend to be those seeking the background to *Measure for Measure*; but, despite its naiveties, it can still engage interest, and in one or two respects it reveals curious lacunae in Shakespeare's play.

Shakespeare's possible debts to Whetstone are numerous. He follows Whetstone in seeking to interlink the high drama of the main plot with the sometimes comical social entanglements of the sub-plot, and like Whetstone he rightly blurs the distinction between such plot-levels by showing how the new era of supposedly stern justice involves high and low alike. Instead of Lamia, the courtesan, and her pimp Rosko, the familiars of Phallax, he offers Mistress Overdone and Pompey, the familiars of Lucio. In both texts, the brothel world is shown to be extensive and to have some resilience in adapting to changed circumstances, even though Overdone, like Lamia eventually, seems to be put out of business. Whetstone's hangman, gloating over the apparel he gains from victims, has a more macabre counterpart in Abhorson, a similar inheritor of apparel. Duke Vincentio's choric speech, 'He who the sword of heaven will bear', follows in part the sentiments of King Corvinus's speech in Part 2, I.viii.8–22. Vincentio is called the 'duke of dark corners': a phrase which perhaps echoes the proverbial 'veritas non querit angulos' ('truth does not seek dark corners') uttered by Corvinus in Part 2,III.iii. At the dénouement of *Measure for Measure*, Isabella, at the Duke's instigation, utters her public accusations against Angelo, and investigation follows, even though the Duke is already fully aware her charges are justified; at the dénouement of *Promos and Cassandra*, Cassandra must utter publicly to the King her charges against Promos, even though the King has previously heard them privately and believed them. Although Whetstone does not use the phrase 'measure for measure', the theme is strongly emphasized in his play, and Rosko's remark: 'who others doth deceyve,/Deserves himselfe lyke measure to receyve'[75] sums up many of the main ironies of the action. The proverbial *cucullus non facit monachum* ('the cowl does not make the monk') which is used in *Measure for Measure*, V.i.261, appears in *Promos and Cassandra* as 'A holie Hoode makes not a Frier devoute' (Part 1, III.vi).[76]

Some other possible continuities in characterization are worth noting. Andrugio's sweetheart, Polina, obviously has Julietta as counterpart, and both make clear their penitence for their 'sin'; but Polina may also have contributed some details to Mariana, for both are seen as mourning or mournful, and Mariana's moated grange may have been suggested by Promos' decree 'that the mayde which sin[n']d, should ever after lyve/In some religious house, to sorrowe her misdeede' (2, III.iii).[77] Whetstone's Shrieve has some similarity in role to Escalus, and his merciful Gaoler to the Provost. As we have seen, Shakespeare adopts Whetstone's dramatic device whereby Isabella (like Cassandra) pleads for the corrupt deputy while still believing that her brother is dead. However, comparison soon reveals one of Shakespeare's major innovations. In Whetstone's play, Promos is an ageing man (grey-haired) who becomes infatuated with Cassandra. Angelo seems mature but markedly younger than Promos, and it is stressed that he has appeared to be a cold precisian, a person of a rather puritanical and repressive nature. Promos does not have this reputation, but Shakespeare may have developed the implications of the speech in which Promos (like Angelo) makes clear that his dark sexual desires have been aroused not by any conventional female charms but by the confrontation with patent virtue:

> *Happie is the man, that injoyes the love of such a wife!*
> *I do protest, hir modest wordes hath wrought in me a maze.*
> *Though she be faire, she is not deckt with garish shewes for gaze;*
> *Hir bewtie lures, hir lookes cut off fond sutes with chast disdain.*
> *O God, I feele a sodaine change that doth my freedome chayne.*[78]

As Shakespeare systematically made Angelo a more chilly and repressive figure, so he systematically made Isabella an appropriate counterpart to him. Whetstone's Cassandra is no novitiate, and Promos extends to her the possibility (though one unlikely to be realized) that he may marry her after she has submitted to his sexual desires. By presenting Isabella as a novitiate, Shakespeare both heightens the intensity of her dilemma and the irony of her relationship with 'outward-sainted' Angelo.

Indeed, it is clear that in general Shakespeare has intensified almost every aspect of the source-play: the poetry, the characterization, the psychology and the ironies. While discarding many of Whetstone's characters and plot complications, Shakespeare has enriched and deepened incisively the remainder, giving much more vivid and extreme alternations between scenes and situations. The intensification which results from poetic intelligence is easily illustrated. With Promos' speech, quoted a few lines ago, compare an equivalent speech from Angelo:

> *Can it be*
> *That modesty may more betray our sense*
> *Than woman's lightness? Having waste ground enough,*
> *Shall we desire to raze the sanctuary*
> *And pitch our evils there? O fie, fie, fie!*
> *What dost thou, or what art thou, Angelo?*
> *Dost thou desire her foully for those things*
> *That make her good?.....*
> *O cunning enemy, that, to catch a saint,*
> *With saints dost bait thy hook! Most dangerous*
> *Is that temptation that doth goad us on*
> *To sin in loving virtue. Never could the strumpet*
> *With all her double vigour, art and nature,*
> *Once stir my temper: but this virtuous maid*
> *Subdues me quite. Even till now*
> *When men were fond, I smil'd, and wonder'd how.*
>
> (II.ii.168–75, 180–87)

The flexible rhythms and the rapidly associated metaphors make this speech psychologically so much more expressive than that of Promos; and repeatedly the figurative diction enriches, reinforces and extends the moral paradoxes and ironies of the situation. Shakespeare simultaneously gives a much stronger sense both of the private individuality of the character and of the general implications (psychological, moral and religious), for others and perhaps for us, of his plight. The religious imagery of Angelo's speech (the razed sanctuary, the 'cunning enemy' who baits his hook with saints, the temptation to 'sin in loving virtue') supports Geoffrey Bullough's claim:

> Consideration of the play in relation to its sources and analogues . . . . . suggests that Shakespeare conceived the theme in terms more religious than his predecessors. He accentuated points in their work which based the story in a society whose values . . . . . were preponderantly Christian, in principle if not in practice. To make Isabella a novice and the Duke to disguise himself as a friar, were not entirely necessary, but once accepted these devices bring consequences which affect the tone of the play.

Nevertheless, Bullough concluded, '*Measure for Measure* is not a "Morality" but a romance interwoven with threads of sociology and ethics'.[79]

In Whetstone's play, some of the names have the inconsequentiality of most names in everyday life, while others are type-names, Morality-play names which give an intermittent sense of moral fable or allegory to the action. Such type-names include that of the prostitute, Lamia (*lamia* being Latin for 'witch or sorceress'); Phallax (*fallax* being Latin for 'false or deceitful'); and Rapax (*rapax*: 'rapacious'). In Shakespeare's play, as we have seen, there is a similar mixture, some names being relatively inconsequential and others (Vincentio, Abhorson) being relatively symbolic. Both Shakespeare and Whetstone are drawing in part on the legacy of those forms of drama (the Morality play and, long before that, the Roman drama) in which stylization of names is common. The more a literary work strives to be realistic, the more the names of characters may have the inconsequentiality of everyday nomenclature; and the more it is non-realistic (e.g. allegoric or symbolic), the more the proper names themselves will be symbolic. In Shakespeare's plays, it is generally the case that the majority of proper names are non-symbolic, but the proportion varies according to the nature of the work. Thus, in the relatively realistic *Hamlet*, the name Fortinbras ('Strong-arm') is appropriate to the active warrior who will eventually inherit the kingdom, but other names lack such resonance; whereas in the relatively symbolic *The Tempest*, Prospero, Miranda, Caliban and Ariel all have appropriately resonating names. In *Measure for Measure*, the proportion of symbolic names, and the degree to which the symbolic possibilities of the names should guide interpretation, are matters of critical debate; but the example of *Promos and*

Cassandra, as well as of Shakespearian plays before *Measure for Measure,* indicates the need for a flexibility in responsiveness and a recognition that an inconsistency or variability of convention is to be expected. The speech by Angelo which we considered a minute ago has shown that Shakespeare's richly metaphoric diction, and the readiness of his characters to oscillate between self-examination and generalization about human nature, enable Shakespeare to fuse the concrete and the abstract, the particular and the general, and thus to reconcile in the very texture of the verse the respective strengths of the realistic and the symbolic modes.

A final point to be made about Whetstone's *Promos and Cassandra* is that its ethical discussion, while lacking the intensity and splendour of that in *Measure for Measure,* does reveal certain interesting lacunae or omissions in Shakespeare's play. Andrugio, like Claudio, is sentenced to death even though his act of copulation was not that of a lecher but rather that of a lover with his betrothed. His sister, Cassandra, repeatedly and emphatically makes the point that the law against fornication has obviously been 'wrested much amiss':

> *The lecher fyerd with lust is punishèd no more*
> *Than he which fel through force of love, whose mariage salves his sore.*
>
> (1; II.i)

To Promos she says:

> *Weigh, Weigh, that Mariage works amends for what committed is.*
> *He hath defilde no nuptial bed, nor forcèd rape hath mov'd,*
> *He fel through love, who never ment but wive the wight he lov'd.*
> *And wantons sure to keepe in awe these statutes first were made,*
> *Or none but lustfull leachers should with rygrous law be payd.*
>
> (1; II.iii)

When we turn to *Measure for Measure* and examine Isabella's plea for Claudio, we see an important lacuna in her arguments. She does not, as Cassandra had done, make the important point that the law has been 'wrested much amiss'; rather, she fully accepts that the law has been justly applied, and bases her plea mainly on the ground that the vigour of justice should be tempered with mercy. There are various possible explanations of this change. One is that it is true to character: Isabella is a rather puritanical and in some ways immature novitiate who has sought 'more strict restraint' even at her priory, so she is less likely to discriminate between the sexuality of lovers and of lechers. Another is that Shakespeare had such ample repositories of sexual disgust in his imagination that he himself sometimes blurred the distinction: as we have seen, Claudio's imagery is initially surprisingly pejorative when he is defining his own sexual conduct. And another is technical: that Isabella's failure to discriminate between different circumstances of copulation has the dramatic function of enabling Angelo to use her own arguments against her when he offers her his sexual ultimatum. Lastly, one commentator has suggested that Isabella is unaware that Juliet and Claudio were united by a private though unsacramental marriage contract (a *sponsalia de praesenti*), for Lucio had told her only 'Your brother and his lover have embrac'd'; and her consequent ignorance of their contracted state makes her plea to Angelo the more general one of lenity to lechery, which again facilitates the dramatic irony of Angelo's demand.[80]

A related shift in emphasis can be seen in the matter of the compelled loss of chastity. Whetstone gives fuller presentation to the argument that a compelled deed is not a heinous deed. Andrugio says to Cassandra:

> *Nay* Cassandra, *if thou thy selfe submyt,*
> *To save my life, to* Promos *fleashly wyll,*
> Justice *wyll say thou dost no crime commit:*
> *For in forst faultes is no intent of yll* .....
> *Knowe forcèd faultes, for slaunder neede not care* .....
>
> (1; III.iv)

The King himself, on hearing her tale, adopts the same view:

> Cassandra, *take comfort in care, be of good cheere:*
> *Thy forcèd fault was free from evill intent,*
> *So long, no shame can blot thee any way.*
>
> (2; III.iii)

Nevertheless, after her enforced loss of chastity, Cassandra dons the blue gown of the fallen woman and complains that she is guilty of 'synne' and has lost her honour; and the King insists that Promos shall marry her 'For to repayre hir honour'. The physical fact of maidenhead has, for many centuries (for religious, cultural and economic reasons), carried such potent symbolic associations with feminine virtue that such an ambiguous attitude to the loss of Cassandra's virginity is easily understandable.[81] At least Whetstone makes clear that the ancient equation of physical maidenhead with virtue can reasonably be challenged by the more pragmatic and enlightened view that the woman remains innocent if her loss of chastity is compelled. In *Measure for Measure*, this latter idea gets short shrift from Isabella. When Claudio says,

> *What sin you do to save a brother's life.*
> *Nature dispenses with the deed so far*

> *That it becomes a virtue*[,]

Isabella furiously replies:

> O, you beast!
> O faithless coward! O dishonest wretch!
> Wilt thou be made a man out of my vice?
> Is't not a kind of incest, to take life
> From thine own sister's shame? . . . . .
>   Take my defiance,
> Die, perish!

> (III.i 133–9, 142–3)

The violent, passionate and almost hysterical quality of this response is emphasized by the contrast with Cassandra's measured reply to Andrugio's argument:

> *How so th'intent is construed in offence*
> *The Proverbe saies, that tenne good turnes lye dead,*
> *And one yll deede, tenne tymes beyonde pretence,*
> *By envious tongues report abrode doth spread.*
> Andrugio *so my fame shall vallewed bee,*
> Dispite *wyll blase my crime, but not the cause.*
> *And thus although I fayne would set thee free,*
> *Poore wench, I feare the grype of slaunders pawes.*

> (1; III.iv.)

Cassandra's reasoning is altogether more pedestrian and prudential. The extremity of Isabella's response suggests not only a more vital and passionate character, but also a very paradoxical one: though about to dedicate her life to the virginal contemplative world of the cloister, she reveals a startling power and involution of sexual imagining. A loss of her virginity to save a brother's life she at once intuits as a form of incest: a sexual act that generates a living brother from a sister. It is one of those scenes in which a Shakespearian character seems to anticipate and invite psychoanalytic commentaries. Again, Shakespeare's adaptation of Whetstone heightens the sense of dramatic stress and conflict by accentuating temperamental and ethical contrasts and thus making a solution through compromise seem unattainably remote. Above all, comparison with the worthy but pedestrian Whetstone makes evident Shakespeare's supreme combination of articulate intelligence, sensitivity and imagination.

(iii) The Substituted Bedmate

In *Measure for Measure*, Angelo copulates with Mariana, who loves him and wishes to marry him; but he believes that he is copulating with an

Isabella who does not love him and is submitting only under duress. At the instigation of the Duke, Mariana has secretly taken Isabella's place in bed with Angelo. This device is known as 'the bed-trick' or 'the substituted bedmate'; and its use in *Measure for Measure* is one of the most controversial features of the play.

Some commentators have regarded the device as morally repugnant, and therefore a major defect in the work. (Quiller-Couch said that Isabella thus becomes 'a mere procuress'.) Others have claimed that this is an ancient and traditional element, and one which Shakespeare's audiences would have regarded as entirely acceptable. Furthermore, worthy figures in the play either justify it morally (as the Friar-Duke does) or fully accept its propriety (as Isabella and Mariana do); so we should adopt a coolly historical perspective. A third view is that though Jacobeans were not troubled by it, we are, since we, morally, are more enlightened.[82] A fourth view, to which I incline, is that (here as elsewhere) the text is its own best critic. D. H. Lawrence once said:

> The degree to which the system of morality, or the metaphysic, of any work of art is submitted to criticism within the work of art makes the lasting value and satisfaction of that work.[83]

This applies to *Measure for Measure*. In solving one set of problems, Shakespeare created another set; and though he diligently strove to resolve the new ones, some of the more intelligent and powerful parts of the text establish a defiant resistance to the resolution.

As we have noted in the previous section, in all the main sources of *Measure for Measure* the counterpart to Isabella does indeed copulate with the counterpart to Angelo. But in developing the character of Isabella, Shakespeare made her so much the strong-willed novitiate, so much a person who responds with utter revulsion to Angelo's lustful demand, that a salutary plot-development became necessary. So the Duke was put in a position to intervene, and the basis of the intervention is his knowledge that Mariana exists and retains love for Angelo, her erstwhile suitor. These two major innovations in the story, one being the active clandestine presence (instead of the absence) of the ruler, the other being the availability of a surrogate sexual partner, cause some new problems. The first is that the very active, inquisitive and manipulative Duke is not easy to reconcile with the evidence that the Duke was formerly rather shy, retiring and contemplative. Another difficulty is that the introduction of Mariana as a character in the play seems tardy: no mention is made of her until the plot seems imminently to require her presence, so the reader may suspect

Shakespeare of unpremeditated improvisation.[84] The main problem remains the propriety of the bed-trick itself.

W. W. Lawrence argued, quite rightly, that there were many precedents in folk-lore and popular tales for the basic device of the substituted partner.[85] (There was biblical warrant: Genesis X X I X :16–26.) It figured in such well-known collections as Boccaccio's *Decameron* and Painter's *Palace of Pleasure*; and R. S. Forsythe's *The Relations of Shirley's Plays to the Elizabethan Drama* lists twenty-one plays of the period which employ the device. It was even believed to take place in real life and, significantly, was termed 'a virtuous deceit': Francis Osborne's *Memoires* referred back to

the last great *Earle of Oxford*, whose *Lady* was brought to his bed under the notion of his *Mistris*, and from such a virtuous deceit she [the Earl of Pembroke's wife] is said to proceed.[86]

When Shakespeare wrote *Measure for Measure*, the device was fresh in his memory, because he had used it in his previous comedy, *All's Well That Ends Well*. There his main source had been the story of Giletta of Narbonne in *Decameron*, Day I I I, Tale 9, which he may have read in the French translation by Antoine le Maçon as well as in the English version by William Painter. In *All's Well That Ends Well* (in which the main plot follows Boccaccio's narrative quite closely) Helena is married, by the King's decree, to Bertram. Bertram is scornful and says that he will accept her as his wife only 'When thou canst get this ring upon my finger, which never shall come off, and show me a child begotten of thy body that I am father to'. Subsequently he attempts to seduce Diana, his hostess's daughter; and Helena, learning of this, takes Diana's place in bed with Bertram and duly acquires the ring and becomes pregnant, so that eventually Bertram is obliged to acknowledge her as his wife indeed.

In the case of *Measure for Measure*, Shakespeare's development of the intransigent character of Isabella appears to have obliged him to depart from his main sources so as to incorporate a bed-trick resembling that in *All's Well That Ends Well*. The Duke (as Friar) explains to Mariana that since she was formerly betrothed to Angelo, it is not sinful for her to take Isabella's place:

> *Nor, gentle daughter, fear you not at all.*
> *He is your husband on a pre-contract:*
> *To bring you thus together 'tis no sin,*
> *Sith that the justice of your title to him*
> *Doth flourish the deceit*

(I V.i.71–5)

The justification of the act is morally much more dubious than was the case in *All's Well That Ends Well*. There, Helena was fully (in the eyes of the law and the Church) the wife of Bertram, so there the bed-trick meant that a husband was saved from adultery and deceived into consummating a lawful union; and the deception was poetic justice, given the seemingly impossible conditions that Bertram had imposed on her. In emotional terms the act of copulation, though false (Bertram thinking he is copulating with Diana), is less murky than that in *Measure for Measure*, for at least Bertram believes that his partner has chosen voluntarily to embrace him. In *Measure for Measure*, however, Mariana is submitting to an act of copulation which, emotionally, in the man's belief, is rape: a compelled act by an unwilling partner who has been forced to comply in order to save her brother's life. In religious terms, too, the act is murkier. The Friar-Duke says ''tis no sin'; but he is wrong. Angelo had entered into a sworn spousal (*sponsalia iurata*) with Mariana; and he had then broken the promise because her dowry was lost and because (he alleged) she was guilty of dishonourable conduct. But such a spousal could not lawfully be broken unilaterally, and Mariana still loves Angelo. The Duke exploits the rule defined by Henry Swinburne's *Treatise of Spousals* (written around 1600, though not published until 1686): 'Spousals *de futuro* do become Matrimony by carnal knowledge betwixt the Partners betrothed.'[87] In other words, the pledge to marry later (*sponsalia de futuro*) is converted into a present, private marriage (*sponsalia de praesenti*) by the act of sexual intercourse. Nevertheless, the contemporary view was that though such private marriages were binding and valid in the eyes of God, they were still sinful; and the sin could be purged only if, subsequently, a proper church marriage took place. The Duke knows this, for in Act V he says to Angelo:

> *Go, take her hence, and marry her instantly.*
> *Do you the office, friar.*

Furthermore, if the *sponsalia de praesenti* entailed by the sexual intercourse of Angelo and Mariana was certainly sinful in the eyes of the church, it could not even claim validity in the eyes of the law. As Professor Schanzer has explained:

It is doubtful, however, whether a court of law would have ruled that cohabitation with one's bride when taken for another person turned a *de futuro* contract into matrimony. Certainly *error personae*, i.e. marriage contracted with a person mistaken for someone else, was one of the recognized grounds for annulment.[88]

73

The less vigilantly you think about the bed-trick in *Measure for Measure*, the more acceptable it is; and the more vigilantly you think about it, the less acceptable it is. If you're not very vigilant, you may think: 'The Friar-Duke says it's all right; Isabella, who is a militant moralist, says, "The image of it gives me content already." The poetic justice is surely what matters: Angelo, a vicious deceiver, is subject to a benign deception; the end justifies the means, and the end is that Isabella is preserved from rape and Mariana gets her man.' If you are very vigilant, you may think: 'This play has, until the introduction of the bed-trick, been so realistic and so intelligently analytic of moral and sexual matters that it has taught me vigilance; I resist the relaxation into an acceptance of conventional and comic poetic justice that now seems to be invited. The similarity of the Duke (in Friar's robes) to a procurer is somewhat ludicrous; his delight in hatching this scheme and in justifying it seems out of keeping with his role as spiritual guide and mentor, particularly when he is seen to define as sinless what is, according to the Church, sinful. Isabella's deference to the judgement of the "Friar" may be understandable, yet this is a different Isabella from the woman who, not very long ago, was so redoubtable in defying her brother in the name of chastity. Furthermore, the Duke, whose scheme will gratify the lust of a would-be rapist, now seems to be condoning an act far worse than the loving copulation of Claudio and Julietta, which he had regarded as indeed sinful and worthy of most deep penitence. It is undoubtedly part of Shakespeare's intention that in *Measure for Measure* many characters should be seen to learn from bitter experience: this applies to Claudio, Julietta, Angelo, Isabella, and even the Duke himself. The trouble is that the Duke does not seem to learn *enough.* His relish at his own fertility in scheming – his dexterity and quality of rapid glibness – seems to increase progressively towards the dénouement. He reflects gravely about the sins and errors of others, but at no point does he stop to reflect on the lies and distortions – and, indeed, the moral contradictions – which his own plotting has entailed. The reader who relaxes into the Duke's mode of "poetic justice" may be able to enjoy that plotting and the conclusion, but the price paid for such relaxation is a loss of the relatively intelligent engagement that the play elsewhere invites and rewards. And it is noticeable that in recent productions of the play, the Duke's assurances in Acts III and IV that the bed-trick is perfectly legitimate are often greeted by the audience with sceptical chuckles: the incongruity between the garb (that of a Friar) and the gab (that of a sexual entrepreneur) generates a possibly unintended comedy.'

Part 3 The Content of *Measure for Measure*

3.1 The Reliability of the Text

All critical judgements of *Measure for Measure* are based on the surviving early text. In places it is garbled, and it may be incomplete; therefore the foundations of judgement are not fully secure. Modern authors customarily have the opportunity of proof-checking their works as they are printed, but this was an opportunity denied by his circumstances (and also, in this case, by his death) to Shakespeare.

In 1623 the 'First Folio' of Shakespeare's works was published: the first 'collected' edition, with the title *Mr William Shakespeares Comedies, Histories, & Tragedies. Published according to the True Originall Copies.* The contents had been gathered by John Heminge and Henry Condell, two of Shakespeare's fellow-actors. At least half the plays in the volume had previously been published singly in Quarto editions; but eighteen either had not been so published or have not survived in Quarto form, and therefore are available to us only through the care of Heminge and Condell. As there is no surviving Quarto of *Measure for Measure*, editors are dependent on the Folio text, which is believed to have been based on a transcript of Shakespeare's manuscript made by Ralph Crane, the 'scrivener' or secretary of the King's Men. Crane's transcript was then set in type by two, three or four compositors, of whom at least one was a careless workman 'with a tendency to omit words or even lines, to improvise and misread, to confuse verse and prose, and to "justify" by breaking long lines of verse into short ones'.[1] Most modern editors discreetly tidy the text. Although *Measure for Measure* presents no textual problems as great as, say, that of Act V of *The Taming of the Shrew* (which appears to lack a final scene resolving the deception of Christopher Sly), it contains several problematic passages. Three examples follow.

(i) In the opening lines of the Folio text of the play, the Duke says:

> *Of Gouernment, the properties to vnfold,*
> *Would seeme in me t'affect speech & discourse,*
> *Since I am put to know, that your owne Science*
> *Exceedes (in that) the lists of all aduice*
> *My strength can giue you: Then no more remaines*

> *But that, to your sufficiency, as your worth is able,*
> *And let them worke .....* [2]

A standard modern edition (Arden) renders the passage thus:

> *Of government the properties to unfold*
> *Would seem in me t'affect speech and discourse,*
> *Since I am put to know that your own science*
> *Exceeds, in that, the lists of all advice*
> *My strength can give you. Then no more remains*
> *But that, to your sufficiency, as your worth is able,*
> *And let them work.*

(I.i.3–9)

This passage begins lucidly but veers into obscurity at 'But that, to your sufficiency, as your worth is able'. The line is patently corrupt. It does not make grammatical sense in its context, as a main verb is lacking; and it is four syllables too long for a normal line of pentameter: only a rapid gabble can force it into the pattern of five metrical feet. Perhaps a subsequent line is missing, or perhaps the compositor mixed the beginning of one line with the ending of the next. We might say, 'So what? Does a garbled line or two matter much?' The answer is, 'Unfortunately, yes. If the corruption of this line has been rendered conspicuous by unintelligibility, it follows that elsewhere there may be lines whose corruption has been rendered inconspicuous by intelligibility: they make sense, and this disguises the fact that their sense is not that which Shakespeare intended.'

(ii) The Folio text of the Duke's speech at the end of Act III contains the following passage:

> *How may likenesse made in crimes,*
> *Making practise on the Times,*
> *To draw with ydle Spiders strings*
> *Most ponderous and substantiall things?*

The editor of the 1951 Tudor edition renders it thus:

> *How may likeness, made in crimes,*
> *Make a practice on the times,*
> *To draw with idle spiders' strings*
> *Most ponderous and substantial things!*

Although a question has become an exclamation, while 'Making' has been helpfully changed to 'Make a', the passage still presents difficulties. The phrase 'may likeness' remains obscure: editors have variously emended this to 'may that likeness', 'my likeness' and 'may lightness', and have suggested that there might originally have been another couplet between

'Times' and 'To draw', and that 'made' might originally have been 'wade'. In context, the intended gist of the passage seems to be this: 'Some people (like Angelo) are versed in crime and are able to use slender means (lying words) to achieve important ends (e.g. seduction, treacherous execution, and the corruption of authority).' However, fitting the given text to this gist requires some tricky feats of ingenuity. Perhaps the compositor garbled Crane's transcription, or (less likely) Crane's transcription garbled the text of the manuscript, or (still less likely) the manuscript itself was incomplete or erroneous.

(iii) In Act IV, scene i, the Duke has a short soliloquy (five and a half lines, beginning 'O place and greatness!'). Editors note that these lines appear to have been transferred to their present location from an earlier long soliloquy at the end of Act III, scene ii. In sense, the short soliloquy would serve well as the opening of the earlier long one. Possibly these lines were transferred in order to fill a gap created by the loss or censorship of a different soliloquy.

These small editorial cruces have at least one large implication. They reveal the presence of the spirit of chanciness which haunts the transmission of Shakespeare's original words. Conspicuous garbling in one passage implies inconspicuous garbling in others. Furthermore, Shakespeare's love of mixed metaphors and his gradually increasing use (during his quarter-century as a dramatist) of convoluted syntax make it difficult for editors to be certain that an odd metaphoric sequence or a perplexing sentence-structure is necessarily a sign of textual corruption. In general, most critics are obliged to regard as reliable the text as currently established by reputable scholars; but the occasional conspicuous errors and oddities in transmission remind us that if Shakespeare were to come to life today and were to look over our shoulders at the pages before us, he might often say: 'No, those aren't quite my words; my words were more vivid and my sense more lucid than this.' Sometimes (as at the end of *The Taming of the Shrew*) he might say: 'But they've left out a whole scene!'; and at other times (as in the case of the 'doublets' in Acts IV and V of *Love's Labour's Lost*)[3] he might say: 'But they've printed the passages that I'd crossed out!' In the last forty-six lines of *Measure for Measure*, is the silence of Isabella a deliberate reticence, or did an inkstained compositor, turning aside for a swig of ale, overlook and consign to oblivion a few lines in which she gladly accepts the Duke's offer of marriage?

3.2 Implications of the Title

The phrase 'measure for measure' was proverbial before Shakespeare adopted it as a title;[4] and, as the proverb itself could do, the title *Measure for Measure* points in two contrasting directions: both towards sternly retributive justice and towards mercy. The former direction is made clear at V.i.406–9:

> An Angelo for Claudio; death for death.
> Haste still pays haste, and leisure answers leisure;
> Like doth quit like, and Measure still for Measure.

The Duke is speaking: he claims that as Angelo has killed Claudio, so Angelo in turn must die. According to the Duke's gloss, the titular phrase connotes the Old Testament's harsh doctrine, 'life for life, eie for eie, tothe for tothe' (Exodus XXI: 23–5; Leviticus XXIV: 17–20; and Deuteronomy XIX: 21). In Shakespeare's *3 Henry VI*, II.vi.55, Warwick cites the proverb when advocating the beheading of Clifford, the slayer of Rutland: 'Measure for Measure must be answerèd'.

Duke Vincentio's bark is worse than his bite: he knows the New Testament as well as the Old. The merciful implication of the title *Measure for Measure* also has clear biblical warrant.

Ye haue heard that it hath bene said, An eye for an eye, & a tooth for a tooth.
But I say vnto you, Resist not euil: but whosoeuer shal smite thee on thy right cheke, turne to him the other also.

(Matthew V: 38–9)

Ivdge not, that ye be not iudged.
For with what iudgement ye iudge, ye shal be iudged, and with what measure ye mette, it shal be measured to you againe.

(Matthew VII: 1–2)

Iudge not, and ye shal not be iudged: condemne not, and ye shal not be condemned: forgiue, and ye shalbe forgiuen.
Giue, and it shalbe giuen vnto you: a good measure, pressed downe, shaken together and running ouer shal men giue into your bosome: for with what measure ye mette, with the same shal men mette to you againe.

(Luke VI: 37–8)

Thus, while the Duke uses the phrase 'measure for measure' to mean 'death for death', symmetrically retributive justice, its source in the New Testament plainly lends it a related yet contrasting association: be merciful if you wish to receive mercy. The play gives, locally, strong advocacy to both claims: Angelo's arguments at II.i.27–31 and II.ii.100–105 are severe but logical and consistent. What emerges as its conclusion to the debate, however, is no simple advocacy of 'turning the other cheek', even though it is clearly no advocacy of ruthless retribution. What emerges is a blend of paternalistic authoritarian policy, ideas of mercy and lenity deriving from the New Testament, and the 'poetic justice' of theatrical comedy – in which, traditionally, the retribution is ironically apt yet lenient and constructive. (Laws which seem rigid at the beginning of *Love's Labour's Lost* and *A Midsummer Night's Dream* have melted by the end.)

A useful commentary on the resolution has been offered by Elizabeth Pope in *Shakespeare Survey* 2. She surveys the Renaissance discussions of 'measure for measure' and of the balance to be struck between the mercy enjoined by Christ and the duty to maintain law and order in the state, and suggests that the authorities of the day tended to gloss over or blur the extent of the potential contradiction between Christ's teaching and political–judicial practice. *Measure for Measure* dramatizes strongly this element of contradiction and offers what, for the times, was an unconventionally radical resolution:

> [T]he Duke, having summoned Claudio and revealed the truth, proceeds not only to pardon him, but to let off Angelo, Lucio, and Barnardine as well, with penalties entirely disproportionate to what their conduct deserved by ordinary Renaissance standards.
>
> We may, if we please, argue that Shakespeare suddenly remembered he was writing a comedy and decided he had better botch up some sort of happy ending to send the audience home contented, regardless of probability and doctrine alike. But all the evidence goes to show that the audience would have left for home equally contented – perhaps even more contented – if Angelo, Lucio, and Barnardine had been punished, like Shylock, or remanded for judgement at some future date, like Don John in *Much Ado about Nothing*. And when we recall the special difficulties and defects of Renaissance doctrine, it seems at least possible that the conclusion of *Measure for Measure* may rather represent a deliberate effort – perhaps a little clumsy, certainly romantic – to 'do something' about that disturbing discrepancy between the concepts of religious mercy and secular justice.[5]

3.3 The Plot

The following sub-section offers a stark plot-summary which endeavours to be 'neutral' or non-evaluative in tone. In 3.32 I discuss some of the notable and problematic features which even such a basic plot-summary may reveal. One of these features, the inconsistent time-scheme, receives separate attention in sub-section 3.33.

3.31 *Conventional Plot-Summary*

Act I. Scene i

The Duke prepares to make a rapid and unpublicized departure from his city, Vienna. He delegates power to Escalus, who is to be Angelo's aide, and to Angelo, who is to act as deputy and is advised to reconcile 'Mortality and mercy'. Angelo asks to be tested more fully before such a responsibility is placed upon him, but the Duke overrules his request: he has been chosen after mature consideration.

I.ii

We learn that Angelo has vigorously implemented the old laws against immorality. Lucio's bawdy chatter with two gentlemen is interrupted by the entry of Mistress Overdone, the brothel-keeper, who complains that Claudio has been arrested and sentenced to death for having impregnated Juliet; and Pompey, a procurer, reports the proclamation that all brothels in the suburbs are to be demolished. Lucio talks to the remorseful Claudio, who explains that he and Juliet had entered into a marriage contract and were only awaiting the arrangement of a dowry before proceeding to a religious wedding-ceremony. The new enforcement of the old law (which prohibits sexual union before holy wedlock) means that Claudio is indeed subject to the death penalty. He therefore asks Lucio to visit Isabella (Claudio's sister) and beg her to intercede for him.

I.iii

The Duke explains to Friar Thomas the reasons for his temporary retirement. As the laws have fallen into disuse, so licence and disorder have increased; and, since the Duke was responsible for that situation, it is proper that someone else – Angelo – should have the task of enforcing the laws anew. Secondly, the Duke wishes to find out what Angelo's nature really is; at present he seems coldly puritanical. So, disguised as a friar, the Duke will remain secretly in Vienna, watching and assessing.

I.iv

Lucio visits Isabella, a novitiate at a nunnery, and tells her of her brother's plight; she agrees to petition Angelo on behalf of Claudio.

II.i

Escalus asks Angelo to be merciful to Claudio, arguing that Claudio is of good family and has succumbed to a temptation so common that even Angelo may have experienced it. Angelo replies that ''Tis one thing to be tempted . . . . . ,/Another thing to fall'; the law must take its course, and Claudio must be executed by the next morning. There follows the long, ludicrous and confused hearing of the case against Master Froth and Pompey Bum. Constable Elbow, while practising unnatural intercourse with the English language, explains that Pompey is a pimp and Froth one of his clients. Pompey defends himself by means of prolix obfuscation. Angelo impatiently departs from the hearing, leaving Escalus to resolve the matter: Pompey is dismissed with a warning to mend his ways, while Elbow is tactfully invited to seek a replacement for himself. Justice (a remarkably taciturn character) remarks that Angelo is severe.

II.ii

Isabella visits Angelo and, prompted and encouraged by Lucio, sues for mercy for her brother. She argues that many people have committed, without penalty, Claudio's offence; Angelo replies that if the law had operated strongly, those people would not have dared to offend: Claudio's death will set a salutary example. She then stresses the arrogance and hypocrisy of human authorities and suggests that if Angelo has ever felt a temptation like Claudio's, he should be merciful. Angelo wavers ('She speaks, and 'tis such sense/That my sense breeds with it') and agrees to hear her again on the following day. When she leaves, Angelo reflects bitterly that though in the past he felt immune from sexual temptation, the modest and virtuous Isabella has aroused his lust.

II iii

The Duke, disguised as friar ('Friar Lodowick', we later learn), visits the prison and commends Juliet for her penitent frame of mind.

II.iv

At the second interview granted to Isabella, Angelo says that he will spare Claudio only if she agrees to submit to Angelo's sexual desires. She is slow to understand his proposal; when she does so, she declares that if Angelo does not pardon her brother, she will proclaim to the world Angelo's wickedness; but he retorts that his denial and unstained character will be more convincing than her allegation. Isabella reflects that Claudio would rather die than let her be dishonoured.

III.i

The Duke (as friar) visits Claudio and persuades him to face death stoically. With the Provost, the 'friar' then withdraws to eavesdrop on the ensuing conversation between Claudio and Isabella. She tells Claudio of Angelo's offer; after initially resigning himself to death, Claudio considers with increasing anguish its impending reality, and begs her to submit to Angelo. She upbraids him indignantly. The 'friar' then speaks privately first to Claudio, asserting that Angelo's offer was merely a test of her virtue and never a real opportunity to evade death, and secondly to Isabella, unfolding an ingenious plan. Once Mariana was betrothed to Angelo, and still loves him though she was jilted by him; if Isabella pretends to acquiesce in Angelo's lustful scheme, Mariana can (concealed by darkness) take her place in bed with Angelo; thus both Isabella's honour and Claudio's life can be saved, while Mariana will be advantaged.

III.ii

The Duke, still disguised as friar, upbraids Pompey, who has again been arrested as a procurer. Lucio declines to provide bail for Pompey, and during conversation with the 'friar' alleges that the Duke has been a drunken lecher. Escalus and the Provost enter, sending Mistress Overdone on her way to jail. She complains that Lucio informed against her, even though she has looked after his illegitimate child, born to Kate Keepdown after he had broken his promise to marry her. Escalus reassures the 'friar' about the good character of the Duke and expresses concern for Claudio. The Duke, alone, reflects on the hypocrisy of Angelo and asserts the need to use craft against vice.

IV.i

The 'friar' introduces Isabella to Mariana, to whom he has long been a counsellor, and who is persuaded to take Isabella's place at the clandestine meeting with Angelo. The 'friar' assures Mariana that since she is betrothed to Angelo, copulation with him will be 'no sin'.

IV.ii

At the prison, the Provost introduces Pompey to Abhorson, the executioner; Pompey is to be his assistant the next morning, when Claudio and Barnardine (a convicted murderer) are to be executed. The 'friar' hints to the Provost that Claudio's death sentence may soon be countermanded; but when the message from Angelo then arrives, far from countermanding the order, it reinforces it: Claudio must be executed by 4 a.m. and his head sent to Angelo. The 'friar' (producing a letter from the Duke, to lend authority to his words) instructs the Provost to keep Claudio secretly alive while executing Barnardine and sending Barnardine's head to Angelo instead of Claudio's.

IV.iii

Pompey, Abhorson and the 'friar' attempt to summon Barnardine to execution; he firmly rejects the summons, being drunk and unprepared. The Provost tells the 'friar' that one Ragozine, a pirate, has now died of fever at the prison; his head could be sent in place of Claudio's. The 'friar' agrees, and says that Barnardine, as well as Claudio, should secretly be kept alive. Vincentio plans to send letters to Angelo instructing him to meet the Duke on his return the next day. Isabella arrives at the prison to inquire after her brother; the 'friar' tells her that Claudio has been executed, and that she should take a letter to Friar Peter, who will bring her before the Duke the next day so that she can denounce Angelo publicly. Lucio tells the 'friar' how he once perjured himself to the Duke so as to evade marriage to the pregnant Kate Keep-down.

IV.iv

At court, Escalus and Angelo discuss the Duke's strange letters, which command them to surrender their authority at the city gates on the Duke's arrival. Angelo, alone, reflects guiltily on his presumed misdeeds: the deflowering of Isabella and the execution of Claudio.

IV.v

The Duke instructs Friar Peter, who is helping him to gather friends for the public ceremony.

IV.vi

Isabella expresses misgivings to Mariana about the 'friar's' plan, according to which Isabella (and not Mariana) must accuse Angelo of fornication with her.

V.i

In a public place near the city gate, the Duke is welcomed by Angelo and Escalus; he thanks them for their good work during his absence. Isabella now appeals for justice, alleging that Angelo is a treacherous murderer and a 'virgin-violator' to whom she had been forced to yield. The Duke denounces her for slandering Angelo, orders her to be taken to prison, and demands that 'Friar Lodowick' (who has apparently conspired with Isabella) should be summoned for questioning. Friar Peter says that Mariana can refute Isabella's accusations. Mariana enters to declare that it was she herself, not Isabella, who copulated with Angelo; Angelo declares that he hasn't been near Mariana for five years. The Duke goes out, leaving Angelo and Escalus to inquire into these 'slanders' and detect whatever conspiracy may have instigated them. 'Friar Lodowick' then enters to denounce Angelo; Escalus, encouraged by Lucio, orders him to be seized and tortured on the rack to discover his subversive purposes. The Provost and Lucio attempt to arrest the 'friar'; in the struggle with Lucio, his hood comes off and the Duke stands revealed. Angelo, confronted, immediately confesses his guilt and begs for speedy death. First, the Duke commands that Angelo must immediately be married to Mariana; next, when they return from the rapid ceremony, he insists that Angelo must die, since he had executed Claudio. Mariana begs for Angelo's life, and, in response to her appeals, Isabella herself seeks clemency for him. The Provost fetches both Barnardine, who is freed by the Duke, and another prisoner, who is discovered to be the living Claudio. The Duke pardons Claudio, proposes marriage to Isabella, and spares Angelo; while Lucio, after first being threatened with death, is sentenced to marriage to Kate Keep-down. Finally, the Duke reminds Claudio to 'restore' by wedlock the 'wrong'd' Juliet, blesses the match of Angelo and Mariana, thanks Escalus and the Provost, and repeats his offer of marriage to Isabella. The company departs for the palace.

3.32 Comments on the Plot-Summary

There are many ways of searching or scanning a play. A reader or beholder may, for a while, give priority to the basic story, or the characterization, or the imagery; to the problem areas, the areas of oddity or obscurity, paradox or contradiction; to the theatrical effects – the visual, iconic or strikingly dramatic moments; or to the tension between the expected and the unexpected, the conventional and the unconventional. The most comprehensive and informative mode of scansion may well be a moral scansion – provided that the term 'moral' be interpreted in a very capacious and flexible way, to take note óf all the kinds of valuation that a text commends (kinds which in turn should be submitted to the reader's valuation). A full 'moral' appraisal should consider both big and small effects, surges and ripples of feeling, both explicit commendations and the tacit commendations operating through image, inflection, syntax, vocabulary; and such an appraisal will inevitably have its political implications. One complicating factor is that good literary works will in part (by their complexities and innovations) challenge the bases of customary moral and political judgements. Another is that since fiction, however realistic, is never interchangeable with non-fictional reality (literary daggers never draw real blood), the sense of refuge, escape or holiday from practical ethics plays against the ethical attention the works solicit.

A scan which is focused on the paraphrasable plot may be more useful in drawing attention to what it excludes than in what it includes. The previous plot-summary of *Measure for Measure*, as it stands, may have some limited value for a novice; it may help to guide him or her, at the first reading, through the unfolding narrative. It may also have some limited value for a person who has read the play already but needs a simple reminder of some of its features. Although virtually every critical discussion of the work (however sophisticated or selective) entails reference to its plot, a plot-summary alone is practically useless as an indicator of merit. Reduced to a brief synopsis, a tragedy becomes indistinguishable from a third-rate melodrama, and a vivid satire resembles an implausible farce.

The synopsis omits or conceals the shocks and surprises, the intensities, the shifts in tone and mood, the vitalities of the contrasting individuals, the diverse richnesses of embodiment. It gives disproportionate space to complicated manoeuvres. The relationship between the synopsis, the full text and the play in performance is, perhaps, analogous to the relationship between a small drawing of a skeleton, a film of a living person, and a direct observation of that person. Juxtaposition of the three will reveal some resemblances; but simultaneously it emphasizes the huge disparities.

The summary may at least draw attention to some of the thematic ironies of the action. One important theme is that of vicarious action. As A. D. Nuttall has argued, this is developed 'in a very pretty sequence of variations meeting in a final resolution':

For example, one may hear the theme in brilliant *accelerando* if one traces that strand of the plot which brings Lucio into contact with the Duke. In III.ii Lucio slanders the Duke to the Friar, not knowing that the Duke and the Friar are one and the same person (though he seems to know that the Duke has disguised himself). Then, at V.i.130f., he slanders the Friar to the Duke, not knowing – again – that they are the same person. Thus Lucio's fertility in slander is frustrated by the Duke's fertility in subterfuge. The variety of the Duke's appearances cancels out the variety of Lucio's mendacity, leaving a single net offence – the slander of a prince.

Again, the theme of vicarious action is intricately linked to the theme of interrupted betrothal:

The venial sin of Mariana in sleeping with her betrothed formally echoes the venial sin of Claudio who slept with *his* and so began the whole chain of events. The stratagem of Isabel and the Duke mathematically cancels out the stratagem of Angelo, who is brought to commit the very crime for which he had sentenced Claudio . . . . . ; and the double falsehood issues in a strange propriety. Thus we have a peripeteia [i.e. reversal] within a peripeteia.[6]

The synopsis, as Nuttall's comments suggest, draws attention to the ironic analogical structure of *Measure for Measure*. Shakespeare has very deliberately introduced a range of similarities in situation to engage us in a comparative consideration of differences in effect. He gives us not just one instance of an interrupted or retarded progress to full wedlock, but three instances: Juliet's, Mariana's and Kate's. There is not one instance of pregnancy before proper marriage, but two instances: Juliet's and Kate's. We see not just one person confronted by imminent execution, but four persons: Claudio and Barnardine in Acts III and IV, Angelo and Lucio in Act V. Three justices, and not one or two, have their patience tested by the Pompey/Froth hearing: Angelo, Escalus and Justice. It is this complicated comparative system which helps to give such analytic intelligence to the play.

When referring to the Duke in his guise as friar, my synopsis termed him a 'friar', using quotation marks to denote the fact that this is only an assumed role. Consistency in this use of quotation marks required a conscious effort. In Shakespeare's (and in many Elizabethan and Jacobean) plays there is a standard non-realistic convention that disguise is always successfully deceptive. Beneath the cowl, the Duke's face cannot be recognized even by Escalus. We readily and rapidly suspend our scepticism about this convention, partly because it is so common and familiar, and partly because our tolerance is richly rewarded by the dramatic consequences, the ironies and discomfitures that ensue in the fictional world. But it is also the case that the adoption of disguise does more than give a character a remarkable power to deceive. It also generates a sub-character or secondary character, as though one person had become a pair of Siamese twins, joined, yet each quite distinct. When Edgar in *King Lear* becomes Poor Tom, the Bedlam beggar, he is so convincing in the role that it is easy, in parts of the play, to forget that he is a disguised Edgar and to believe in him indeed as a tormented lunatic whose utterances stem naturally from the maelstrom of wild turmoil at the centre of the Lear-world. Similarly, when the Duke becomes 'friar', it is as though he is generating a sub-character which at times (for example in III.i) takes on a virtually distinct identity and can be regarded almost as Providence incarnate.

The synopsis also draws attention to the problem of the stage-manoeuvring in the last scene. The dénouement or unravelling is peculiarly complicated, generating some tricky stage-movements: for example, the Duke has to appear in his own person, depart so that he can resume his disguise, appear as 'Friar Lodowick' and be arrested, before once more resuming his normal appearance and authority. Isabella has to make a partly untruthful denunciation of Angelo, be rebuked by the Duke's untruthful defence of Angelo, be denounced as a liar by Friar Peter, and contradicted by Mariana, who in turn is abused as a 'pernicious woman' by the Duke. 'Friar Lodowick' must be criticized by Lucio, defended by Friar Peter, denounced and threatened by Escalus, and assailed by the Provost and Lucio. The revelation that Claudio has survived is markedly retarded. Angelo is firmly sentenced to death before being spared; so is Lucio. It can be argued that since the Duke knows all the essential facts before the scene begins, these protracted manipulations are dramatically excessive and induce gratuitous confusions.

Some, but not all, of the deceptions and delays have an obvious moral and psychological function. Isabella has been morally severe and intemperate in the past; believing that he is responsible for the death of Claudio, she has good reason to seek vengeance against Angelo. Had she known that Claudio had survived, it would have been less difficult for her to respond to Mariana's plea. But, after understandable hesitation, she does still respond to it by seeking mercy for Angelo, even though she believes him to be a treacherous slayer. The Duke's concealment of the living Claudio is thus largely justified by the test it provides of Isabella's development towards compassionate fellow-feeling, and the subsequent production of Claudio can seem almost like a miraculously earthly reward for those who obey the divine precept to 'love your enemies'. One of the features which differentiates Shakespeare from other dramatists of his period is his keen interest in the dramatization of extremes of charity, mercy and magnanimity. Immediately before Isabella kneels to make her plea, the Duke tells a harsh lie to accentuate the severity of her test: of Angelo he says, 'He dies for Claudio's death.' Sentimentality is averted by the concisely argued defence of Angelo that she offers:

> *I partly think*
> *A due sincerity govern'd his deeds*
> *Till he did look on me .....*
> *His act did not o'ertake his bad intent .....*

It is also consistent with her previous attitude to Claudio's 'sin' that she talks of Claudio's love-making and Angelo's lust as though they differed only in the fact that Claudio fulfilled his desire whereas Angelo did not.[7]

The testing of Isabella does not, however, explain and vindicate the vertiginous scale of the complications of the last scene. Here, reference to the ending of *All's Well That Ends Well* is helpful. The last scene of *All's Well* has a similarly vertiginous sequence of accusation and counter-accusation, similarly accelerating towards an act of apparent injustice. There Diana (whose place in bed with Bertram had been taken by his wife, Helena) falsely accuses Bertram of having copulated with her, and she asserts that Helena's ring, worn by Bertram, is her own and was given to him by herself. (Diana has been instructed by Helena to make these allegations.) Diana then denies she gave the ring to Bertram. At this point, the patience of the King, who has been endeavouring to discover the truth, becomes exhausted and he grows angry.

KING   *This ring was mine, I gave it his first wife.*
DIANA   *It might be yours or hers for aught I know.*
KING   *Take her away, I do not like her now;*
             To prison with her .....
             Unless thou tell'st me where thou hadst this ring,
             Thou diest within this hour.
DIANA   *I'll never tell you.*
KING   *Take her away .....*
             Wherefore hast thou accus'd him all this while?
DIANA   *Because he's guilty, and he is not guilty.*

> *He knows I am no maid, and he'll swear to't;*
> *I'll swear I am a maid, and he knows not.*
> *Great king, I am no strumpet, by my life;*
> *I am either maid, or else this old man's wife.*
KING   *She does abuse our ears; to prison with her.*[8]

From the beginning of the play, it has been established that the French King is a wise, kindly figure, the central upholder of justice in this fictional world. Yet the complications in the last scene are so great, and are presented in such a giddying way, that even this wise and benevolent figure becomes confused and impatient, and, in his impatience, begins to act unjustly and intolerantly: he is at the point of having the innocent Diana thrust into prison when at last Helena, and clarification, arrive. There is, thus, a combination of protracted dramatic suspense and a moral warning. The suspense is protracted because the audience expects a steady progress towards clarification and a happy ending; instead, the revelations initially lead to confusion and the scene veers towards an unhappy ending, before the true dénouement tardily appears. The moral warning is implicit in the presentation of the King, which shows that even those who normally are reliable upholders of justice may, when matters become bewilderingly complicated, react angrily and unjustly, jumping to the wrong conclusion.

The same double process – protracted dramatic suspense coupled with a moral warning – is at work in the last scene of *Measure for Measure*. Here the trustworthy figure is Escalus, who throughout the play has been a voice of honesty and moderation. Nevertheless, rather as the complicated sequence of accusation and counter-accusation had bewildered the French King and goaded him into intolerance, so Escalus, baffled and annoyed, is driven into angry injustice:

ESCALUS   *Why, thou unreverend and unhallow'd friar!*
> *Is't not enough thou hast suborn'd these women*
> *To accuse this worthy man .....?*
> *Take him hence! To th'rack with him! – We'll touse you*
> *Joint by joint, but we will know his purpose.*
> *What! Unjust! .....*
> *Away with him to prison! Where is the Provost? Away with him to prison!*
> *Lay bolts enough upon him: let him speak no more. Away with those*
> *giglets too, and with the other confederate companion!*
>   (V.i.303–5, 309–11, 342–6)

And it is at this point that the Duke and real clarification appear.

So in both plays, Shakespeare displays an interest in a spiralling dénouement which at first moves strongly in the direction of confusion and injustice before veering at last into clarification and justice; and, in both, a trustworthy authority is tested by complexity to breaking-point. Escalus, who had managed to remain clearheaded and judicious throughout the comic complications of the Pompey/Froth hearing, fails to do so when confronted with the far graver complications of the Mariana/ Isabella/Lodowick hearing. His error is readily understandable, for some of the claims he must adjudicate are deliberately cryptic and paradoxical. Just as, in *All's Well*, Diana had presented riddling evidence –

> *Because he's guilty, and he is not guilty.*
> *He knows I am no maid, and he'll swear to't;*
> *I'll swear I am a maid, and he knows not.*

– so, in *Measure for Measure*, had Mariana's evidence shared the riddling style of folk-tales' formulae, and repeated that pun on carnal and rational 'knowing':

> *My lord, I do confess I ne'er was married;*
> *And I confess besides, I am no maid.*
> *I have known my husband; yet my husband*
> *Knows not that ever he knew me.*

The moral implication of each sequence, in *All's Well* and *Measure for Measure*, is the same: confusing evidence may tempt even the worthy judge into injustice; therefore, when in perplexity, err on the side of mercy. And, dramatically, both sequences offer a historical lesson for modern audiences. They remind us that in Elizabethan and Jacobean drama, there was a taste for a dénouement which was ingenious rather than economical and realistic. As the revenges in revenge drama sought to be cunningly spectacular rather than briskly functional, so the dramatists, pulled now towards realism and now towards the teasingly intricate, often preferred the latter in the final act of a play. If the final moments of *King Lear* seem savagely and unconventionally realistic, this is partly because, earlier in the same scene, the action had modulated towards the formally ingenious (and folkloric) with the disguised Edgar's formal challenge to, and duel with, Edmund, followed by the production of Goneril's letter and the remarkably rapid deaths of Goneril and Regan. In *Measure for Measure*, the very conspicuous mixture of realism and stylization has been one source of the divisions amongst the critics (who often seek to make texts more consistent than they really are); but what is thus presented, somewhat more conspicuously than usual, is a tension which is ubiquitous in drama of that time. Just as rhymed and blank verse co-existed with prose, so stylized plotting co-existed with realistic plotting; and our judgement is complicated by our recognition of the elements of stylization within the prose and within the 'realism'. Criticism of *Measure for Measure* has long been perplexed by the problem of discrimination between a flexible and an acquiescent response, or between a judicious and an intolerant response; and Shakespeare, who customarily offers critical anticipations of his critics, has made this very problem a central subject of the play.

3.33   *The Time-Sequence*

In some of his plays, notably *The Comedy of Errors* and *The Tempest*, Shakespeare could maintain a taut and consistent time-scheme; but more frequently the chronology in his plays is loose, flexible and even inconsistent. As early as 1693, Thomas Rymer, in his *A Short View of Tragedy*, drew attention to what was subsequently termed the 'double time-scheme' of *Othello*. Iago, tempting Othello into jealousy of Cassio, talks as though several weeks at least have elapsed since Desdemona's marriage; and for Othello's jealousy to have plausibility, we too must imagine this to be the case. Yet (excluding the voyage from Venice to Cyprus, which is irrelevant to the matter, since Cassio and Desdemona voyaged in separate ships) the main action takes less than three days, and offers no opportunity for the sustained adultery that Iago alleges. After their marriage, Othello and Desdemona spend two nights together (though they are interrupted); and on the third night, he kills her. Shakespeare has so firmly compressed the diffuse time-span of the source-tale that a split develops between the chronology of enactment and the chronology of motivation. In theory, this inconsistency destroys the basis of the plot; in practice, audiences are generally untroubled by it, mainly because their interest in the immediate drama overrides their sense of the calendar.

Othello presents in extreme form an inconsistency between the chronological 'foreground' and 'background' that we find elsewhere. In *Love's Labour's Lost*, for example, the main events seem to span two days, but some subsidiary events (particularly if we believe Costard's allegation in V.ii.661–3 about Jacquenetta's pregnancy by Armado) span weeks and months. *Measure for Measure* offers a kindred inconsistency. The main dramatic events concerning Claudio, Angelo and Isabella (from the time of Claudio's arrest to the public return of the Duke) seem to take only four or five days at the most; in I.ii.61–3, Overdone says that Claudio is to be executed 'within these three days'. The period of the Duke's supposed absence appears to be one of months rather than days: he is thought to have travelled as far as Poland (I.iii.14), Rome, or even Russia (III.ii.85–6); and in his guise as 'Friar Lodowick' he becomes well established, paying frequent visits as adviser to Mariana (IV.i.8–9). We may reconcile this long span with the short span of the central action by assuming that a month or two elapse between the Duke's departure and the arrest of Claudio. However, the tribulations of Overdone and Pompey, which begin at the time of Claudio's arrest, imply a longer time-span than is appropriate to Claudio's desperate plight. In I.ii.85–103, the conversation between Pompey and Overdone suggests that they will have to uproot their brothel trade and establish new premises elsewhere; but within a few hours of the same day (according to the central time-scheme) their new 'hot-house' is well established (II.i.63–5), and Pompey has been arrested; and in III.ii, ostensibly only one day later, Pompey is re-arrested after further exploits in his vocation as ponce. Thus we gain the impression of a double chronology: an action which lasts a few days takes simultaneously several weeks or even a couple of months.

'These anomalies are intentional, and serve an artistic purpose,' says J. W. Lever.[9] Suspense is maintained by our sense that the Duke must act very speedily to save Claudio from death and outwit Angelo's machinations, while the long-time references enable us to believe that Angelo's rule has been fully established and its many consequences unfolded. The anomalies seem to matter little: human memory is fallible, and we concentrate in the play on 'human interest' rather than on details of clock-time or calendar-time. Another reason is that whereas when reading a realist novel or a modern detective story we accept a basic chronological consistency as a necessary convention (and are alert to chronology because the authors themselves often make it important), we soon learn that Elizabethan and Jacobean texts are often casual or flexible in temporal matters, so we lower our expectancy of close consistency. An imagination which can accept that a stage is at once a stage and a fictional Vienna, now its court and now its prison, can accept a double time-scheme – provided that the dramatist rewards us, in exploration of experience, for our tolerance. It is the straitjacket of the three neoclassical unities (of time, place and action) which needs defence, rather than the rich freedom of Shakespearian drama. Indeed, a double time-scheme reminds us that in everyday life we experience time as multiple and contradictory: the mechanical clock says one thing, the mental clock (varying its pace in pleasure and pain, retrospection and anticipation, dreaming and waking) says another.

3.4 Characterization

3.41 *The Part-List*

The First Folio gives the following list of parts:

Vincentio: the Duke.
Angelo, the Deputie.
Escalus, an ancient Lord.
Claudio, a young Gentleman.
Lucio, a fantastique.
2. Other like Gentlemen.
Prouost.
Thomas. ⎫
          ⎬ 2.Friers.
Peter.   ⎭
Elbow, a simple Constable.
Froth, a foolish Gentleman.
Clowne.
Abhorson, an Executioner.
Barnardine, a dissolute prisoner.
Isabella, sister to Claudio.
Mariana, betrothed to Angelo.
Iuliet, beloued of Claudio.
Francisca, a Nun.
Mistris Ouer-don, a Bawd.

This list omits the Justice, who speaks in II.i, Varrius, a mute presence in V.i, the Boy, who sings in IV.i, and possible silent supporting roles: lords, officers, citizens and servants.

Some of the names are arbitrary, some are clearly significant, and others are possibly significant. 'Vincentio' means 'conquering' or 'conqueror', which is appropriate to the Duke's eventual triumph over corruption. 'Angelo', in its root-meaning of 'messenger', has some appropriateness to a man who delivers the Duke's edicts to the people; and its subsequent meaning, 'angel, divine attendant', has ironic aptness for one who took pride in his virtue and fell into moral darkness: 'Let's write good angel on the devil's horn', says Angelo (II.iv.16). 'Escalus' is a name that Shakespeare had previously used in *Romeo and Juliet*: there, a corruption of 'della Scala', it was given to the Prince who restores order. 'Claudio' was a name given in *Much Ado About Nothing* to a young Florentine lord.

The cast-list describes Lucio as 'a fantastique' – a fop or foolishly affected character. The name probably derives from the Latin noun *lux* (light); and Shakespeare frequently associates the noun 'light' (illumination) with the adjective 'light' (meaning 'wanton' or 'sexually promiscuous'): an association which fits this character. 'Elbow' is given two explanations in the text: the hapless constable explains, 'I do lean upon justice'; and when he is lost for words, Pompey remarks that the constable is 'out at elbow'. Someone whose sleeve is out at elbow (worn through) is exhibiting a sign of impoverishment; Elbow is impoverished in wit, as he is, perhaps, in means. 'Froth' is obviously appropriate to a superficial and unsubstantial fellow. The 'Clowne' is better known as Pompey Bum, whose name exercises the facetiousness of Escalus in II.i.209–16. 'Bum' aptly means 'sham or fraudulent', as well as 'buttocks'. 'Abhorson' combines 'abhorrent' and 'whoreson'. 'Barnardine' is a name whose root-meaning is sometimes given as 'bear-hard', i.e. 'hardy as a bear', which is not inappropriate for this character of 'stubborn soul'. 'Isabella' is cognate with 'Elizabeth', and seems an arbitrary choice to me (the narrator of the source-story in Whetstone's *Heptameron* is an Isabella); but Roy Battenhouse postulates 'devoted to God' as its appropriate root-meaning. Again, 'Mariana' seems familiar and arbitrary as a name-choice, but Battenhouse postulates the root-meaning as 'bitter grace'.[10] The name 'Juliet' defies etymologists, but the heroine of *Romeo and Juliet*, like her namesake in *Measure for Measure*, found that a private betrothal had dire consequences. 'Francisca' is saintly enough for a nun. 'Ouer-don' ('Overdone') will do nicely for a 'bawd of eleven years' continuance' who was 'Overdone by the last' of her nine husbands.

3.42 *The Main Characters*

Not surprisingly, one of the dominant themes of *Measure for Measure* is that of 'the testing and education of a character by means of harsh experience'. This is not surprising, because it is a theme virtually universal in literary texts, as indeed it is in life. Nevertheless, *Measure for Measure* offers a strikingly wide range of characters who illustrate this theme. Claudio and Juliet, Overdone and Pompey, Angelo and Isabella, Escalus and the very Duke himself are subjected to harsh experience, and their 'educability' is assessed within the play. Even the Duke's final concern for Barnardine exemplifies the theme's importance:

> . . . . . *pray thee take this mercy to provide*

> *For better times to come. Friar, advise him;*
> *I leave him to your hand.*

What the play obviously suggests is that the moral worth of a character depends not so much on any absence of vice or folly as on the ability of that character to recognize vice or folly in himself or herself and to be educable in the direction of mature virtue. In the hierarchy of conscience and educability, Angelo, for all his vicious corruption, ranks higher than the jauntily and recalcitrantly immoral Pompey. The isolation of individual characters for consideration should not conceal from us their interactive functions – the ways in which each forms part of a complex comparative structure.

1 The Duke

Interpretations of the play as a whole tend to hinge on interpretations of the Duke's character. Most of the evidence for a favourable interpretation is so prominent as to need little explication: he has carried out a 'controlled experiment' in seeing laws reinforced and in testing Angelo and other figures; he has worked hard, in disguise, to avert dishonour and bloodshed; and he imposes a final justice which is firm but merciful. Furthermore, at the close of the play his authority and wisdom are generally endorsed by the comments of the other main characters. He himself, moreover, has been tested and has learnt lessons during the course of the action. He becomes ready for marriage, no longer talking as though love and marriage are for lesser mortals; he has been surprised and ruffled by the slanders of Lucio, has been frustrated by the recalcitrance of Barnardine, and has briefly been caught out by the unexpected ruthlessness of Angelo. A relatively hostile reading of the Duke's character could claim to be either extrapolating features of the text or challenging its premises. In the former case, the reader might claim that if the Duke's former leniency caused social problems, his final leniency is likely to renew them; that the Duke behaved dishonourably in making Angelo bear the burden of enforcing (at his ruler's command) the new stern edicts; and that the Duke's use of disguise and deception, though largely justified by results, was sufficiently Machiavellian to render us remarkably sympathetic to the slanderous Lucio. The Friar-Duke's intentions may be benevolent, but his tone (as at III.i.165–9) often lacks considerate sensitivity to his protégés. A hostile reading which apparently challenges the premises of the text would be one which says that the very principle of an autocratic authority which so manipulates its subjects to secure its position is a political principle from which, for good democratic reasons, we should recoil. Actually, this judgement has some qualified support in the texture of the work and (as we noted in section 2.4) in Shakespeare's treatment elsewhere of calculatingly successful rulers, whose efficiency curbs engaging exuberance.

The characterization modulates to accommodate different functions: sometimes the modulation is from realism to stylization, as when the Duke speaks chorically on the role of the responsible ruler (III.ii.254–75); and sometimes, when the Duke is disguised as Friar, the role of 'Friar Lodowick' approaches independent status. Lastly, we should note that Vincentio, who is certainly an actor and a director, resembles a playwright. As the Friar-Duke finds that some individuals may awkwardly resist and complicate his plotting, so Shakespeare may have found that the logic of individual characterizations could awkwardly resist and complicate his intended plot structure. Vincentio's mixture of planning and improvisation may be analogous to that of Shakespeare, who must occasionally have said (like Iago), ''tis here, but yet confus'd'.

2   Angelo

Angelo's inconsistencies are consistent: psychologically the characterization has coherence, subtlety and power. His sexual puritanism is not that of someone who lacks sexual drives but rather that of someone who possesses them but has sought to keep them in check; similarly, his staunch dedication to the severe laws is not that of someone who is naturally authoritative but that of someone who has inner weakness to conceal. His inflexibility entails brittleness; a willed, strained quality. If his attempted coercion of Isabella, his treacherous treatment of Claudio and his hypocritical denunciation of Mariana and Isabella invite our hostility, there are some mitigating qualities: he is reluctant to accept the responsibility the Duke offers him, asking for 'some more test' of his worth to be first made; he is tormented rather than gratified by his own lust and its consequences; and, when eventually exposed, he seeks 'Immediate sentence, then, and sequent death'.

Dramatically, the scene of his first encounter with Isabella (II.ii) is probably the finest in the play – intensely and cogently argued, and with expanding ironies: a novitiate arguing for lenity to lechery, and a 'precisian' defending moral severity while experiencing the first strong sexual temptation of his life. The point at which he seems to relent is powerfully ironic:

ISABELLA   *Merciful Heaven,*
Thou rather with thy sharp and sulphurous bolt
Splits the unwedgeable and gnarlèd oak,

> Than the soft myrtle. But man, proud man,
> Dress'd in a little brief authority,
> Most ignorant of what he's most assur'd –
> His glassy essence – like an angry ape
> Plays such fantastic tricks before high heaven
> As makes the angels weep; who, with our spleens,
> Would all themselves laugh mortal.

LUCIO [to Isabella] *O, to him, to him, wench! He will relent;*
> *He's coming: I perceive't.*

PROVOST [aside]   *Pray heaven she win him.*

If Lucio is correct in perceiving signs of Angelo's relenting at that point (and the context suggests strongly that he *is* correct), the ironies are at once ethical and psychological. First, the eloquence of her case has been so strong as to challenge almost any case for stern justice; but, in particular, her reference to 'proud man',

> *Dress'd in a little brief authority,*
> *Most ignorant of what he's most assur'd*[,]

though of general application to sinful and erring humanity, has peculiarly close application to the Angelo whose puritanical assurance may mask inner uncertainty and ignorance; indeed, her arguments, by eliciting a powerfully sexual desire within him, are verifying the ignorance she postulates. In the ensuing scenes, Angelo will become a perfect exemplar of man as 'angry ape', playing

> *such fantastic tricks before high heaven*
> *As makes the angels weep.*

The subsequent dialogue of Isabella and Angelo is one of the finest instances, in Shakespeare's plays, of ironic cross-purposes:

ISABELLA   ..... *Go to your bosom,*
> *Knock there, and ask your heart what it doth know*
> *That's like my brother's fault. If it confess*
> *A natural guiltiness, such as is his,*
> *Let it not sound a thought upon your tongue*
> *Against my brother's life.*

ANGELO   *She speaks, and 'tis such sense*
> *That my sense breeds with it. – Fare you well.* [Going.]

ISABELLA *Gentle my lord, turn back.*

ANGELO *I will bethink me. Come again tomorrow.* [Going.]

ISABELLA *Hark, how I'll bribe you: good my lord, turn back.*

ANGELO *How! Bribe me?*

ISABELLA *Ay, with such gifts that heaven shall share with you.*

LUCIO [to Isabella] *You had marr'd all else.*

ISABELLA	*Not with fond sickles of the tested gold,*
	Or stones, whose rate are either rich or poor
	As fancy values them: but with true prayers,
	That shall be up at heaven and enter there
	Ere sunrise: prayers from preservèd souls,
	From fasting maids, whose minds are dedicate
	To nothing temporal.
ANGELO	*Well: come to me tomorrow.*
LUCIO [to Isabella]	*Go to: 'tis well; away.*
ISABELLA	*Heaven keep your honour safe.*
ANGELO [aside]	*Amen.*
	For I am that way going to temptation,
	Where prayer's cross'd.
ISABELLA	*At what hour tomorrow*
	Shall I attend your lordship?
ANGELO	*At any time 'fore noon.*
ISABELLA	*Save your honour.* [Exeunt all but Angelo.]
ANGELO	*From thee: even from thy virtue!*

Like someone trying to evade a temptation, Angelo twice tries to leave, and twice is called back by Isabella. Her mention of a bribe has a double connotation for him: the suggestion of a monetary bribe, and the hint of a sexual bribe: the irony of the latter misconstruction being emphasized by her subsequent stress on the purity of the 'bribe' – 'prayers from preservèd souls,/From fasting maids, whose minds are dedicate/To nothing temporal.' Again, her piously respectful parting remark, 'Heaven keep your honour safe' (i.e. 'May heaven safeguard your honourable self'), is ironically interpreted by Angelo as 'May heaven safeguard your virtue from temptation'. She repeats the courteous formula: 'Save your honour'; and Angelo, alone, completes the prayer: 'From thee: even from thy virtue!' – his words summing up the paradox of his plight and giving a double resonance to that word 'virtue'. Her moral fervour has become for him, perversely, a sexual challenge; and thus she possesses 'virtue' in a different, less ethical sense – a distinctive power, particularly the power to engender (as in Chaucer's 'Of which vertu engendred is the flour'), so that her 'sense' can indeed make his sensuality 'breed'.

Dramatically and psychologically, then, this is perhaps the finest scene in the play, and one which gives Angelo a convincing complexity as a character. In Act II, scene iv, he sees Isabella again, and delivers his sexual ultimatum to her; thereafter, as the Friar-Duke comes to dominate the action, the focus of attention tends to move away from concentration on Angelo's divided nature. There is, however, an important soliloquy in Act IV, scene iv:

ANGELO   *This deed unshapes me quite; makes me unpregnant*
          And dull to all proceedings. A deflower'd maid;
          And by an eminent body, that enforc'd
          The law against it! But that her tender shame
          Will not proclaim against her maiden loss,
          How might she tongue me! Yet reason dares her no,
          For my authority bears so credent bulk
          That no particular scandal once can touch,
          But it confounds the breather. He should have liv'd,
          Save that his riotous youth, with dangerous sense,
          Might in the times to come have ta'en revenge
          By so receiving a dishonour'd life
          With ransom of such shame. Would yet he had lived.
          Alack, when once our grace we have forgot,
          Nothing goes right; we would, and we would not.

Here Angelo is experiencing a mixture of guilt, remorse, fear, calculation
and rationalization. Isabella has the power to denounce him, but he
reasons that she will be deterred from using that power not only by her
modesty, which would flinch from proclaiming her loss of virginity, but
also by his high moral reputation, which would deny credibility to her
allegation. When Angelo seeks to justify to himself the killing of Claudio,
he argues that had Claudio lived, he might have taken revenge on Angelo
for the defloration of Isabella. Yet, as one commentator has remarked,[11]
'there is an awkwardness in the expression which seems to betray the
presence of a contrary idea': the ambiguous phrase, 'ta'en revenge/By so
receiving a dishonour'd life', does permit a subsidiary meaning to be
perceived: 'If he had lived, his youthfully riotous nature might subsequently have taken revenge on *him* for being ransomed so shamefully,
the revenge being the subsequent acceptance of a reprobate way of life.'
The subsidiary meaning is faint, but it accounts for the convoluted syntax,
and it is true to two facets of Angelo's character: true to the Angelo who
voiced horror at 'these filthy vices' of Claudio; and true to the Angelo
who sought to discern in others the source of his own misdeeds ('Is this
her fault, or mine?/The tempter, or the tempted, who sins most, ha?').

   In short, the characterization is of a kind that invites commentators to
discuss Angelo as though he were a living human being with credibly
complex motivation. Such a convention of discussion is natural, proper
and economical; only an obtuse literalist would add, 'But of course he is
not a real person; his character is an illusion generated by mere words.'
L. C. Knights once argued, influentially, that too much emphasis had
been placed on 'character' in Shakespeare: '*Macbeth* is a poem,' Knights

said, postulating that work's affinity with *The Waste Land*.[12] Nevertheless, Shakespeare was a dramatist, constructing plays whose characters inevitably invite comparison with, or bring to mind, living people; and Knights's own fine discussion of the thematic riches of *Macbeth* was given co-ordination, to a greater degree than he realized, by his sense of the 'personalities' of the different speakers. (When, in one speech, the English forces are represented as impurities, he remarks that this 'need not surprise us since Macbeth is the speaker'.) Samuel Johnson long ago elucidated the matter: 'Imitations produce pain or pleasure, not because they are mistaken for realities, but because they bring realities to mind.'[13]

3   Isabella

For more reasons than Angelo can perceive, Isabella makes a peculiarly apt counterpart to him in the play. As characterization, she has a similar depth and complexity, and there are some parallels in their psychology. Isabella at the convent wishes for 'a more strict restraint/Upon the sisters'; and some reasons for that hankering after greater restraint and discipline than even the convent gives are indicated in her subsequent exchanges with Angelo and Claudio: a passionate, sensuous nature emerges from her initially reserved and cautious self. In response to Angelo's apparently hypothetical question about her readiness to sacrifice her virginity to save her brother, she replies:

> . . . . . *were I under the terms of death,*
> *Th'impression of keen whips I'd wear as rubies,*
> *And strip myself to death as to a bed*
> *That longing have been sick for, ere I'd yield*
> *My body up to shame.*

The obvious sense is that she would welcome death rather than submit to dishonour; but the terms in which she portrays the approach to death are powerfully and disturbingly sensuous: 'Th'impression of keen whips I'd wear as rubies'; 'strip myself to death as to a bed/That longing have been sick for'. The images do not subvert her intended meaning, but they do complicate it by revealing a sensuous intensity of imagining which indicates forces elsewhere held in check. The same quality is apparent in the fervour of her rebuke to Claudio: 'Is't not a kind of incest, to take life/From thine own sister's shame?' In Act II, scene ii, it is a related quality of fervency, of a response which, under stress, blazes with passionate energy, that unwittingly awakens Angelo's dormant lust. This is not to say that her piety is to be reduced, on Freudian lines, to some 'sublimation' of repressed sexuality. One of the glories of the text is the glowing, lucid eloquence of her pleas for Christian mercy.

ANGELO   *Your brother is a forfeit of the law,*
                And you but waste your words.
ISABELLA   *Alas, alas!*
                Why, all the souls that were, were forfeit once,
                And He that might the vantage best have took
                Found out the remedy. How would you be
                If He, which is the top of judgement, should
                But judge you as you are? O, think on that,
                And mercy then will breathe within your lips,
                Like man new made.

In response to Angelo's curtness surges forth this speech which, as dramatic utterance, seems convincingly spontaneous, cogently expressed, intensely felt; wholly in character, and drawing immense moral authority from the centuries of New Testament teaching which its terse, almost colloquial compression makes immediate. The twelve words, 'And mercy then will breathe within your lips,/Like man new made', are glossed thus by the Arden editor:

Redemption is a second creation of man in God's image. As Adam was given a soul when the Creator breathed life into his nostrils, so the new Adam is redeemed from the first Adam's sin by the breath of divine mercy in Christ, which moves on his lips when he speaks mercifully to his fellow men.

The gloss is accurate; but all that meaning has been conveyed in twelve simple words given at the end of a speech which has been rhythmically resurgent and has reached its climax of momentum at this point. The speech enacts what it claims: she herself is an instance of the 'man new made' when divine mercy breathes within the lips. The Isabella who once, at the convent, had replied to Lucio haltingly and diffidently ('My power? Alas, I doubt') has now revealed a fuller and profoundly devout self; and it is not the least irony of this speech that she herself, in response to Mariana's plea, will eventually let mercy breathe within her own lips on behalf of the very man whom she is now addressing. The intensity of her recoil from Angelo's offer, the fury of her reproach to Claudio's suggestion that she might submit to Angelo, and the fervency of her denunciation of the deputy on the Duke's return: all these make credible her long delay before kneeling alongside Mariana. Her commitment to mercy is the more compelling for her initial, instinctive attraction to forms of retaliatory justice; there has even been a moment in which she responded to Angelo's threat with a form of blackmail of her own:

> *Sign me a present pardon for my brother,*
> *Or with an outstretch'd throat I'll tell the world aloud*
> *What man thou art.*

(II.iv.151–3)

If her acquiescence in the Friar-Duke's employment of Mariana as sexual surrogate with Angelo seems ethically questionable and partly inconsistent with her previous recoil from Angelo's proposal, it can be argued that Isabella is consistent in accepting the authority of a person she knows and trusts as a spiritual adviser, and that a degree of social diffidence before authority was evident in the initial uncertainty of her first encounter with Angelo, when Lucio's prompting was crucial in eliciting her inner fervour. And if numerous critics have expressed dissatisfaction with the intrigues and manoeuvres by which the Duke attains his ends, perhaps one source is that same ethical fervour of Isabella's. So powerfully belittling is her evocation of the 'angry ape' – 'Man, proud man,/Dress'd in a little brief authority' – that even the Duke, exposed to the radiance of her Christian vision, may momentarily appear a little apish, playing his fantastic tricks.

The ethical range of *Measure for Measure* is partly, in the imagination responding to its imagery, a matter of visual and spatial range: of perspectives which now thrust to the foreground the needs and drives of the individual, and now present the individual as part of a posturing humanity dwarfed by the immensities beyond. Sometimes there is a rapid and paradoxical mobility in perspectives, as when Isabella tells her brother:

> *O, I do fear thee, Claudio, and I quake*
> *Lest thou a feverous life shouldst entertain,*
> *And six or seven winters more respect*
> *Than a perpetual honour. Dar'st thou die?*
> *The sense of death is most in apprehension;*
> *And the poor beetle that we tread upon*
> *In corporal sufferance finds a pang as great*
> *As when a giant dies.*

(III.i.73–80)

Against the perspective of 'perpetual honour', life is a fever of six or seven winters' duration; and the transition to death is not to be feared, since a giant's death-pang is no greater than that of a squashed beetle. Yet the phrasing of her comparison of the beetle with the giant quite naturally invites a reading which contradicts her intended sense: the patent, grammatical meaning of the comparison is: 'To the humble beetle, its death-pang is just as enormous as would be a giant's to him.' The ambiguity of her comparison, then, epitomizes that conflict of attitudes to death which has already been evinced in this scene by the contrast between the Duke's advice to Claudio to treat death as a friend, and Claudio's contrasting vista of life as 'paradise/To what we fear of death'.

4 Claudio

In a play which, thematically, dramatizes extremes (retaliation, mercy; marriage, the brothel; repression, licence; commitment to life, commendation of death), it is appropriate that individual characters should oscillate paradoxically in mood and attitude. This is shown clearly in the character of Claudio who, in Act I, scene ii, first seems to acquiesce in his condemnation by authority but soon argues that this authority is tyrannical; just as, in Act III, scene i, he veers from stoical acceptance of death to desperate recoil from it. Again, there is a consistent inconsistency at work: Claudio can be seen as young, callow, impressionable, uncertain; divided between the sense that to appear noble and honourable he should accept his plight unflinchingly, and the sense that he has been unfairly trapped by the law. The instinctive clutching at life ('Death is a fearful thing.....Sweet sister, let me live') follows soon, but entirely credibly, after his assurance to her:

> *If I must die,*
> *I will encounter darkness as a bride*
> *And hug it in mine arms.*

And when the Friar-Duke has dashed the hope of reprieve ('Angelo had never the purpose to corrupt her; only he hath made an assay of her virtue'), Claudio, his passion spent, reverts again to the stoical: 'Let me ask my sister pardon; I am so out of love with life that I will sue to be rid of it.'

These veerings of attitude may not make an impressive character, but they make a credible one; and they are in keeping with the tone of the whole work, in which rapid transitions in viewpoint maintain our engagement with the vitality and complexity of the issues. We may notice, however, that when the Duke finally enforces his own 'viewpoint', the text grants to Claudio not one word of joy or relief at his reunion with his sister.

3.5   Prominent Themes, Images and Terms

3.51   *Themes*

One dominant theme is obviously that introduced by the ambiguous title, *Measure for Measure*: the theme of the reconciliation of justice and mercy, and the establishment of a working compromise between the Christian precept of merciful humility and the need for order in the state. Christianity's most radical and altruistic commandments (love your enemies, turn the other cheek, do good to them that hate you) conflict directly with the practice of virtually all political and judicial systems; the conflict is paradoxical when some of those systems seek to derive authority from Christianity; and *Measure for Measure* gives jagged sharpness to the paradox. Mere mortals generate structures of law and order which aspire to impersonality and may oppress mere mortals. A related theme, therefore, is that of 'judging the judges': the law and its administrators (whether the Duke, Angelo, Escalus or the hapless Elbow) are all scrutinized. As we have seen, 'the testing and education of individuals by harsh experience' is a theme whose variations sound in Angelo, Claudio, Juliet, Isabella, Mariana, and eventually in Escalus and Lucio. Sexuality – its values and perils – is another obvious co-ordinator: if sexual licence is associated with disease and exploitation, asceticism and repression are associated with destructiveness and defilement. Perhaps less obvious, but very important as a basis of patterns of comparison, is the theme of 'deputies, substitutes and vicarious action'. Angelo deputizes for the Duke, Isabella's maidenhead is demanded as an exchange for Claudio's life, and Mariana's maidenhead is a substitute for Isabella's; Barnardine's head is intended as a substitute for Claudio's, and Ragozine's head serves as a substitute for Barnardine's and thus for Claudio's. As in any literary work dealing with hypocrisy and deception, 'being and seeming' proves to be an uninformatively capacious thematic heading. The proverb '*Cucullus non facit monachum*' (V.i.261) could be regarded as a kindred thematic statement, given its various possible interpretations and applications within the text. The title of Aldous Huxley's novel, *Ape and Essence*, derives from *Measure for Measure* and could serve as a sub-title to the play.

3.52 *Images and Terms*

Caroline Spurgeon[14] noted the frequency and importance in the play of
semi-comic personifications, such as 'Liberty plucks Justice by the nose',
'Bidding the law make curtsey to their will', and 'make him bite the law
by th'nose'. She claimed that, even by Shakespeare's standards, there
occurred 'an unusually vivid use of concrete verbs and adjectives applied
to abstractions', as in: 'Hooking both right and wrong to th'appetite,/To
follow as it draws'; 'Lent him our terror, drest him with our love'. A
related quality is the comic-grotesque: 'The baby beats the nurse, and
quite athwart/Goes all decorum'; and 'thy head stands so tickle on thy
shoulders, that a milkmaid, if she be in love, may sigh it off'.

One of the subtlest co-ordinating factors in the text is possibly the
following group of interrelated terms and images. Their common feature
is a degree of ambiguity or flexibility which enables them to refer now to
the sexual and now to the non-sexual.

(a) Pregnancy

Literal pregnancy is conspicuous in the play: the 'mutual entertainment'
of Claudio and Juliet 'With character too gross is writ on Juliet': so in
stage productions she is normally seen to be bulgingly pregnant. Kate
Keep-down does not appear on stage, but her past impregnation by Lucio
is mentioned in several scenes. Pregnancy in the metaphoric sense ('being
full of knowledge or intelligence') is invoked early in the play. In Act I,
scene i, the Duke notes that Escalus is 'pregnant' with knowledge of the
city and its laws. In IV.iv.18–20, Angelo, after fornicating with (so he
believes) Isabella, reflects:

> *This deed unshapes me quite; makes me unpregnant*
> *And dull to all proceedings. A deflower'd maid . . . . .*

'Pregnant' in the sense of 'evident, obvious' (and perhaps with an under-
sense of 'fruitful in application') is used by Angelo in II.i.23–5;

> *'Tis very pregnant,*
> *The jewel that we find, we stoop and take't,*
> *Because we see it . . . . .*

A related term is 'conception', which Angelo uses metaphorically at
II.iv.6–7:

> *And in my heart the strong and swelling evil*
> *Of my conception . . . .*

(b) Coinage and imprinting

In I.i.16, the Duke asks of Angelo, 'What figure of us, think you, he will bear?' (i.e. 'How well is he imprinted with my image? How effectively will he deputize for me?'). A few lines later he tells Angelo,

> There is a kind of character in thy life
> That to th'observer doth thy history
> Fully unfold

– 'character' meaning 'writing, engraving, inscription'. Angelo, punning on 'mettle' (spirit, courage, integrity) and 'metal', says,

> Let there be some more test made of my metal,
> Before so noble and so great a figure
> Be stamp'd upon it.

In Act II, as he sinks into corruption, Angelo remarks, 'Let's write good angel on the devil's horn'; and soon afterwards, in his debate with Isabella, he refers to unlawful copulation which results in pregnancy as 'Their saucy sweetness that do coin heaven's image/In stamps that are forbid'. Isabella echoes the metaphor of forgery when telling him, of women, 'we are soft as our complexions are,/And credulous to false prints' (women are easily deceived – and thus made pregnant – as soft metals are easily imprinted by forgers); and this context may lend a momentarily jarring irony to Angelo's phrasing when he asks her to perceive clearly his intentions: 'Plainly conceive, I love you.'

(c) Sense

'Sense' could be a paradoxical term, since it could mean both 'reason, good thinking, awareness, knowledge' and 'sensuality, particularly sexual lust'.[15] In *Measure for Measure*, the context usually makes clear which of these two main directions of meaning is indicated by a particular usage of the word; but its paradoxicality is dramatically emphasized by Angelo's

> She speaks, and 'tis such sense
> That my sense breeds with it.

Here 'such sense' has the dominant meaning 'with such cogent reasoning', and 'my sense' has the dominant meaning 'my sensual desire, my lust'. There is, however, some semantic interchange. Isabella's arguments have suggested the veniality of fornication and the possibility that Angelo might inwardly have experienced the temptation of lust; while Angelo's phrase 'my sense breeds with it' could partly mean 'my mind begins to be impregnated with ideas of lust and schemes for its fulfilment'. His phrasing makes clear the perverse irony that he, the virtuous ascetic, feels challenged to deflower and defile the virtuous novitiate; indeed, his subsequent reflections suggest that much 'sexual' crime is, rather, crime of violence which seeks to conquer by defilement.

(d) Knowing

The verb 'to know' can mean either 'to have cognition of' or 'to have sexual intercourse with'. The latter meaning is ancient and biblical: thus Genesis, Chapter II, verse 25, says: 'And Adam knewe his wife againe, and she bare a sonne'.

Both Mariana and Lucio exploit the ambiguity. Mariana cryptically declares:

> *I have known my husband; yet my husband*
> *Knows not that ever he knew me . . . . .*
> > *that is Angelo,*
> *Who thinks he knows that he ne'er knew my body,*
> *But knows, he thinks, that he knows Isabel's.*
> > (V.i.187–8, 201–3)

And when the Duke consequently asks Angelo, 'Know you this woman?', Lucio promptly interjects: 'Carnally, she says.'

It could be argued that the whole drama is a play on the double sense of the verb, for the action suggests that true cognition of people is provided by insights into their sexual natures, and that such cognition is a source of power over those people. The Duke's investigations as 'friar' give him privileged knowledge of, and power over, Claudio, Juliet, Mariana, Angelo, Isabella, and even Lucio; and one reason for the Duke's smouldering annoyance at Lucio's slanders may be that Lucio offers a parodic version of the Duke's own cognitive logic – for he claims to possess privileged knowledge of the Duke's secret sexual proclivities and therefore of his character as a whole. This partly explains the lingering force both of Lucio's reference to 'the old fantastical duke of dark corners' and of his remark, 'I am a kind of burr, I shall stick'.

3.6   The Implications of Texture

In literary discussions, 'texture' is a capacious term, but when critics use it they are normally referring to the degree of linguistic expressiveness in a given work. If a dramatic speech has a 'rich' texture, it is likely to be vivid and fervent, to possess a sensuous descriptive vigour, and to carry a rhythmic impetus and flexibility which imply the emotional energies of its speaker; consequently, it will reward close analysis and may be isolated for particular praise. If, on the other hand, a dramatic speech has a 'thin' or 'shallow' texture, it is likely to seem unrewarding to close analysis and may be treated relatively disparagingly. This broad evaluative distinction must frequently be qualified, since there will be occasions when a thin texture is psychologically or dramatically appropriate to speaker or occasion; but, in general, judgements of Shakespearian dramatic discourse quite properly imply the superiority of the richly textured.

Crucial to the evaluation of *Measure for Measure* is a textural change which is particularly marked in Act III, scene i; and some critics have defined the precise moment of the transition as that of the Friar-Duke's re-emergence at line 151 of that scene.[16] The relevant passage is this:

ISABELLA [to Claudio]

> *O faithless coward! O dishonest wretch!*
> *Wilt thou be made a man out of my vice?*
> *Is't not a kind of incest, to take life*
> *From thine own sister's shame? What should I think?*
> 140 *Heaven shield my mother play'd my father fair:*
> *For such a warpèd slip of wilderness*
> *Ne'er issued from his blood. Take my defiance,*
> *Die, perish! Might but my bending down*
> *Reprieve thee from thy fate, it should proceed.*
> *I'll pray a thousand prayers for thy death;*
> *No word to save thee.*

CLAUDIO   *Nay, hear me, Isabel.*

ISABELLA *O fie, fie, fie!*
> *Thy sin's not accidental, but a trade;*
> *Mercy to thee would prove itself a bawd;*
> 150 *'Tis best that thou diest quickly.* [Going.]

CLAUDIO   *O hear me, Isabella.*

151 DUKE [Advancing.] *Vouchsafe a word, young sister, but one word.*

ISABELLA *What is your will?*

DUKE *Might you dispense with your leisure, I would by and by have some speech with you: the satisfaction I would require is likewise your own benefit.*

ISABELLA *I have no superfluous leisure; my stay must be stolen out of other affairs: but I will attend you a while.* [Waits behind.]

DUKE *Son, I have overheard what hath passed between you and your sister. Angelo had never the purpose to corrupt her; only he hath made an assay of her virtue, to practise his judgement with the disposition of natures. She, having the truth of honour in her, hath made him that gracious denial which he is most glad to receive. I am confessor to Angelo, and I know this to be true .....*

From the first Act until III.i.150, the play has been gaining moral and emotional force and intensity as its human dilemmas gather momentum and extremity. Isabella's fierce outburst at her brother is startlingly expressive and revealing, and with it the action seems to have reached a tragic impasse: her defiant intransigence appears to doom him to that death whose horrors he had so fervently imagined a few moments earlier. Yet when, at line 151, the Friar-Duke advances with his 'Vouchsafe a word, young sister, but one word', the emotional temperature suddenly falls, and the fervour of eloquent blank verse is abruptly replaced by the banalities of courteous expository prose. And the 'one word' of the Friar-Duke proves to be very many words, contrivedly imparted. Isabella must withdraw while the 'friar', lying fluently, tells Claudio of Angelo's motives; and Claudio must then withdraw while the 'friar' calls forth, and promptly dismisses, the Provost ('What's your will, father?' 'That, now you are come, you will be gone'), so that he can privately, and at considerable length, explain to Isabella how the existence of Mariana provides a means for a happy solution of the dilemma. Although, subsequently in the play, there are various local recoveries of strength, the main emotional impetus is slackened and diffused, and the proportion of memorably expressive speeches declines.

If we are responsive to textures, then, the play may be its own best critic. When the Friar-Duke emerges as manipulator and intriguer, his very prose (initially courteous but soon brisk, confident and insensitively glib) may warn us, by its bathetic lack of resonance in contrast to the previous speeches, that we are to pay a large price in terms of human experience for those manipulations which provide the happy ending. It is almost as though the devices which save characters' lives threaten to drain the play of its poetic life. 'Never trust the artist. Trust the tale,' said D. H. Lawrence.[17] In this case, the tale's texture perhaps says: 'Trust the exploration of the problems: here be truths. Distrust the solution of the problems: here be expedients.'

3.7 The Play in Production

Between the seventeenth and the twentieth centuries, *Measure for Measure* was one of the more unpopular of Shakespeare's plays, both with the critics and with theatregoers. In the period 1779 to 1812, Sarah Siddons gave lustre to the role of Isabella, but during the Victorian era interest declined. In the twentieth century, however, there was a marked revival of interest which accelerated rapidly in the 1960s, and at present the play is clearly, in the eyes of producers or directors, one of the most challenging of Shakespeare's works: every season seems to offer some major new production.

Some of the reasons for this revival of interest are plain. Various barriers of public and private censorship have crumbled, so that what once seemed offensive or embarrassing now seems frank and honest. The eventual humiliation of Angelo and the lenience of the Duke gratify the anti-Puritanical liberalism which became influential in the 1960s and 1970s; the play's cynical notes harmonized well with the diverse tones of cynicism in much of the new drama and fiction of recent decades; and yet the Christian and hierarchic elements of the text (which gained prestige in various commentaries between 1930 and 1960) remained to gratify the pious, the conservative or the dialectically-minded. Above all, the combination of such diverse features in the text made it topically challenging: the play presented living problems, and the theatre, thanks largely to the continuing influence of Ibsen and Shaw, and particularly to the swelling influence of Brecht (who selected *Measure for Measure* for adaptation), was now increasingly hospitable to the problematic. If the term 'problem play', when applied to a Shakespearian text, had once seemed largely pejorative, the influence of Brecht now made it largely honorific. Features of the work which once might have alienated audiences could now be postulated as deliberate 'alienation effects' which could engage audiences. The play offers seemingly erratic or inconsistent features, together with some enigmatic silences or reticences; all the main characters are fallible and deny us easy identification: and these factors give the text an 'openness' which invites the 'closure' of a co-ordinating, unifying interpretation.

Yet the 'closure' provided by a particular director's interpretation may, by its challenge to previous interpretations or to the audience's likely preconceptions, result in an 'opening' of the text for the audience: a recognition of a protean potential. Frequently, the intelligent director of a famous play works polemically. If previous influential productions have emphasized, say, the cynical and sceptical elements of *Measure for Measure*, the director may be inclined to emphasize the Christian and charitable elements; and he may do this not because he necessarily believes that the final importance resides there, but rather because he sees the enlivening value of such an emphasis: it helps to perpetuate the play's life in the imaginations of the community.

Measure for Measure, said Sir Edmund Chambers, is 'bitter and cynical': it 'drags the honour of womanhood in the dust'.[18] If one influential critical tradition (maintained by Coleridge, Chambers, Quiller-Couch and Dover Wilson) has emphasized the 'dark' or 'morbid' aspects of the play, another, which developed strongly in the period 1930 to 1960 (aided by Wilson Knight, F. R. Leavis, Roy Battenhouse and Nevill Coghill) has stressed the Christian allegorical possibilities. On 27 March 1955 I listened to a version of *Measure for Measure* broadcast on the Third Programme of the B.B.C. The producer was Raymond Raikes, who had been advised by Nevill Coghill. Taking as its basis the doctrine of the Atonement and the parables of Jesus, the production used various means to suggest that the Duke was God in disguise and that Lucio was a close relative of Lucifer, the eternal adversary. Heron Carvic's mockingly metallic voice indeed helped to give the impression that Lucio had diabolic insight – particularly when, speaking of the Duke to the 'friar', he said: 'It was a mad, fantastical trick of him to steal from the state and usurp the beggary he was never born to': which seemed to imply sardonic penetration of the disguise. An echo-chamber was employed to give mysteriously numinous authority to the Duke's more choric pronouncements, and the final dispensation of justice seemed to take place not in the streets of Vienna but somewhere between earth and heaven: a joyous background-music was provided by pealing bells and by angelic choirs singing a Magnificat. However, while the broadcast proceeded, I was dutifully following the text page by page, and some of the liberties taken with the text made me sceptical of the interpretation. Not only was there no warrant for those jubilant bells and celestial singers, but also the production had made drastic omissions from Lucio's speeches: the splended 'tilth and husbandry' speech had been excised, as had Lucio's crucial encouragement of Isabella in I I .ii. As these omissions eliminated some of the most genially human aspects of Lucio's character, they called in question the schematic basis of the whole interpretation. From this production, then, a useful rule was deducible: the more an interpretation depends for its consistency on verbal additions to or deletions from the accepted text, the less valid it is. For obvious economic reasons (save time, save money), directors frequently make textual excisions, and no excisions are innocent: a speech which to one director seems mere padding may to another director seem crucial.

Various stage productions in that period stressed the sanctity of the

Duke. Peter Brook's impressive production in 1950 presented Vincentio 'rather as Friar turned Duke than as Duke turned Friar'; while Anthony Quayle's version at Stratford (1956) and Margaret Webster's at the Old Vic (1957) both presented the Duke as wisely authoritative. As late as 1966, Tyrone Guthrie, in a programme note for his production at the Bristol Old Vic, suggested that Vincentio 'is meant to be ..... a figure of Almighty God; ..... the Heavenly Bridegroom ....'.[19]

Action and reaction. After productions which emphasized the divinity or benign authority of the Duke, it was predictable that subsequent productions might portray him as very fallibly human. A particularly interesting silence in the text is Isabella's silence on hearing the Duke's eventual proposal of marriage; and when Jonathan Miller directed the play (Greenwich Theatre, London, August 1975) he filled the silence not with an acquiescent smile from Isabella but with her horrified recoil. Craig Raine's review of this production (*New Statesman*, Vol. 90, p. 230) is so vivid that it deserves lengthy quotation:

[N]othing could be more natural than the acting in Jonathan Miller's splendid *Measure for Measure*. The stylized gestures that go with doublet and hose have been effectively banished by setting the play in late nineteenth-century Vienna: the Elizabethan strut becomes a modern saunter; arms are more often folded than akimbo; hands that normally aspire to an extra digit or two find their way into pockets; characters sit cross-legged or lounge against tables nearly as much as real people. In the gestural silence created (a quiet that implicitly acknowledges the formative influence of television) even the most understated actions can be clearly heard. As Abhorson, the dapper hangman, conducts an inventory of his tools, his methodical pencil ticks as audibly as the clock in a Rolls-Royce. Equally, Jonathan Miller has rejected the vocal mannerisms usually attendant on Shakespearean verse – *accelerando* exit lines on a rising scale that ends with a eunuch's yelp; the arbitrary alternation, in long speeches, of Peter Piper gabble with emphatically elasticated vowels. Here, the actors *think* before they produce their metaphors; they hesitate at the beginning of sentences and start again; they use a normal speaking voice instead of the favoured echo-chamber situated in clangorous sinuses.

Consonant with this overall realism, the Duke is divested of divine overtones. The office he transfers to Angelo is not 'the demi-god, Authority', but a seedy room – furnished with one faded portrait, a metal bin, paper-clips, rubber-stamps and books of regulations. Its eight doors and one secret panel bespeak the character of the Duke. In this setting, Angelo, the complete bureaucrat from his precise gold spectacles to his cheap briefcase, is sexually stirred by Isabella. Not that her person has anything to do with it. Penelope Wilton plays her as a flat-chested, flat-footed nun in black rubber-soled shoes, clutching with purple hands a nasty handbag, into which she claws for a handkerchief to scarify her raw nose. Angelo is turned on by the only thing which could attract him – the different, harsher set of rules she embodies so fervently. The Duke, too, who has pimped for Mariana, responds to her spiritual drabness which eludes his temporal jurisdiction, and the play ends with his summary dismissal of the underlings, so that he, like Angelo, can proposition Isabella. It is like a gloomy Thurberesque variant on the boss and secretary routine: the ugly stenographer in a novitiate's habit retreating in horrified silence from the middle-aged executive in monkish garb.

Clearly, the theatrical interpretation of any text will express the temperament of the director (with his moral, theological or political biases), his dialectical response to other interpretations, and the cultural pressures of his day. A textual reticence (e.g. that silence of Isabella) can provide a challenge and an opportunity. The Coghill–Raikes production gave the impression that Isabella (who formerly, as a novitiate, might have elected to be a Bride of Christ) was now exalted in symbolic union with the Lord Incarnate. The Miller production, in contrast, lets her silent recoil expose not only her own inhibited, repressive nature but also a seedily opportunistic libido in the Duke. In 1984 the Royal Shakespeare Company's version at the Barbican Centre (director: Stuart Burge; Duke: Daniel Massey; Isabella: Juliet Stevenson) filled the silence with Isabella's joyful embrace of a Duke whose genial sexual ardour towards her had previously given him great difficulty in maintaining his Friar's disguise; indeed, this production found a new source of comedy in some interpolated stage-business in which the 'Friar's' private ministrations to Isabella had, on more than one occasion, provided him with an irresistible temptation to embrace her. Thus the way in which the director chooses to dramatize Isabella's response to the Duke's proposal may act as an imaginative fulcrum to the whole conception of the characters of the Duke and Isabella, and so to much of the play; other adjustments will follow, to maximize co-ordination. The legitimacy of the adjustments depends on the degree of respect for the text, when allowance has been made for the facts that the early stage-directions are rather less authoritative than the speeches and that even the speeches occasionally seem corrupt. 'Respect' need not mean 'servility'; but the most effectively innovatory productions of a play are generally those which combine the maximum plausible change of emphasis with the minimum alteration of the words of the text. If the text has to be significantly cut or re-written, the result should be offered as a director's free adaptation, or as a new play 'based on' *Measure for Measure*, rather than as Shakespeare's play.

The remarkable range and variety of recent stage versions of *Measure for Measure* certainly confirm that the play has come to seem attractively problematic to directors. One reason is clear: in some parts of this text (notably in Acts II and III) Shakespeare's co-ordinating imagination is conspicuously creative and radiantly intelligent, whereas elsewhere it

113

seems markedly less so. By letting his own intelligence copulate with Shakespeare's, the director hopes to vindicate or regenerate the integrity of the whole work. He tries to make the text keep its promises. And one of the biggest ironies of the whole endeavour is that this is a play about an unsanctified union and broken promises of betrothal. If some of the stage versions resemble shotgun marriages (between author and director) or illegitimate offspring (the twentieth century having forced its attentions upon the seventeenth), that is not entirely out of keeping with the preoccupations of the play itself; and if other versions offer happier marriages with legitimate offspring, the Friar-Duke would doubtless pronounce his blessing.

Jonathan Miller[20] provides a director's summing-up:

The point is that the act of dramatic interpretation consists of a journey backwards through time in the effort to find some significant historical ground upon which to raise an eloquent representation of human conflict. Success is then rated, not by the degree to which the performance approximates to an entirely unknowable state of Shakespeare's mind, but by the extent to which the text now speaks with more or less coherent vitality . . . . .

We accept without question the successive transformations of scripture throughout the history of painting and see nothing odd, vain or arrogant in a painter who sets his Annunciation in a medieval Flemish town. Shakespeare himself wrought the same changes upon antiquity, not because he arrogantly supposed their stories to be smaller or thinner than his own imagination but because he realized that one of the tasks of art is to overthrow the tyranny of time and to recreate a universe within which the dead converse at ease with the living.

With the passage of time Shakespeare's plays have quite properly assumed the status of myths and it is the honourable fate of all great myths to suffer imaginative distortions at the hands of those to whom they continue to give consolation and nourishment. The story of Oedipus existed before Sophocles changed it again and when Freud incorporated the tale into his theory of family conflict he was merely adding another substantial chapter to a tale whose telling can never be finished. So let it be with Shakespeare.

3.71 *Differences between the Play on the Page and the Play on the Stage*

A stage production of a play may accentuate the prominence of features which already seemed prominent when the play was read; and it may give prominence to features which seemed not at all prominent when the play was read. In this section, I give three examples of the latter effect. When *Measure for Measure* is performed, many of the new emphases will vary from production to production, according to the predilections of the director and the actors; but I think that the following examples may hold good for most performances of the play.

(i) The Opening of Act IV

> SCENE I [A Grange.]
> Enter Mariana, and [a] Boy singing.
>
> Song
>
> *Take, o take those lips away*
> *   that so sweetly were forsworn,*
> *And those eyes, the break of day*
> *   lights that do mislead the morn:*
> *But my kisses bring again,*
> *   bring again;*
> *Seals of love, but seal'd in vain,*
> *   seal'd in vain.*
>
> Enter Duke [disguised].

MARIANA   *Break off thy song, and haste thee quick away;*
Here comes a man of comfort, whose advice
Hath often still'd my brawling discontent. [Exit Boy.]
I cry you mercy, sir, and well could wish
You had not found me here so musical.

When we read the play, we will notice that at the beginning of this scene the location has changed from the prison to a grange, but our main interest in the dialogue may deny us a strong sense of visual contrast. On stage, the different set and the different lighting will accentuate the contrast between Mariana's location (a quiet retreat) and the sombre place of durance that preceded it. The song gains remarkable prominence. When we read the text, we probably read the words of the song rapidly, and do not imagine its music. In production, the music of this melancholy love-lyric is heard, a refreshing melody; graceful lyricism after the anguish, wrangling, slanders and moral severity of the previous scene. We probably read the song casually; when it is sung aloud to music, its duration is lengthened, and the visual surprise provided by its singer and hearer (the boy and Mariana) who are both new arrivals on stage, previously unseen, also lends impact to it.

The song is about someone whose lover was forsworn, unfaithful: so it is appropriate to the plight of Mariana, who was jilted by Angelo. However, when she sees the 'friar' she sends the boy hurrying away before he can begin his second stanza, and apologizes to the newcomer for her indulgence in such music: the song of profane love will be unseemly to him, though it consoles her grief. For the audience, though, that song had been a brief oasis, a glimpse of Arcadia from the city, a voice of youth amid the adult world; a short incursion of a cluster of moods, emotions and, implicitly, of values, which have been previously warded off by the strenuousness, gravity and roughness of the play. That incursion is of the lyrical gentleness, melancholy and yearning of a love which eludes the stern categorizations and analyses by the ethical or legal or religious. It speaks of art's soft modulations of human conflict and desire into innocent pleasure; it is an obedient boy who sings, and no courtesan.

(ii)   The Activity of Lucio

Stage productions make Lucio seem much more prominent and active than he seemed when the play was merely read. One reason for this is that when we are reading we are well aware of the speeches but tend to forget those characters who are present but silent. Lucio is present in every Act, including the whole of Act V; and he is, of course, present throughout the crucial second scene of Act II, when Isabella first encounters Angelo. Even when silent, Lucio may command attention by his grimaces and gestures; and from his first appearance in Act I, scene ii, he has attracted the interest we bestow on characters who are hard to make out, somewhat unpredictable, veering between good and bad, capable of altruism and baseness, of stupidities but also of welcome shafts of intelligence. He is socially mobile, moving between the minor and the major characters, and morally volatile, being both a cynical and prattling representative of the underworld and a shrewd adviser to Isabella in her intercession for Claudio. At a time when authority is becoming morally and legally oppressive, his jaunty scepticism seems reassuringly independent; and his memorably mocking epitomes of Angelo provide the irreverence that Angelo deserves:

> ..... *a man whose blood*
> *Is very snow-broth; one who never feels*
> *The wanton stings and motions of the sense* .....
> (I.iv.57–9)

Some report, a sea-maid spawned him. Some, that he was begot between two stockfishes. But it is certain that when he makes water, his urine is congealed ice; that I know to be true.

(III.ii.104–7)

An important complication occurs when, having mocked Angelo as frigidly sterile, Lucio proceeds to commend the Duke (to the Friar-Duke) as a crafty old lecher:

Ere he would have hanged a man for the getting a hundred bastards, he would have paid for the nursing a thousand. He had some feeling of the sport; he knew the service; and that instructed him to mercy . . . . .
A shy fellow was the Duke; and I believe I know the cause of his withdrawing . . . . .
The Duke yet would have dark deeds darkly answered: he would never bring them to light: would he were returned!

(III.ii.113–17, 127–9, 170–72)

The comedy during this exchange is splendidly mobile and reciprocal. Some of the laughter is directed against Lucio: he is boldly slandering the Duke without realizing that he is speaking to the Duke in person; and he says 'would he were returned' unaware that he is addressing the returned ruler. Nevertheless, in the theatre the comedy seems predominantly to be at the Duke's expense. Firstly, the disguise as friar which the Duke has adopted to give him freedom to eavesdrop has actually trapped him: the biter is bitten; he has to contain his indignation lest he give himself away. Secondly, the claim that 'The Duke yet would have dark deeds darkly answered', though false in its sexual insinuation, is uncomfortably close to the truth as a claim about the Duke's methods, as his present disguise proves. Thirdly, the suggestion that sexual avidity was the cause of the Duke's shy and retiring nature exposes one of the Duke's failings as ruler: he has in the past distrusted the crowds and has been somewhat reclusive. During the course of the play, the Duke learns from experience the importance of being an active and public ruler. Fourthly, in a world in which Angelo, Isabella and the Duke have spoken of fornication as dangerous, sinful and subversive, Lucio's cynicism seems close to humane and liberal common sense:

Why, what a ruthless thing is this in him [i.e. Angelo], *for the rebellion of a codpiece to take away the life of a man! . . . . .*
Marry, this Claudio is condemned for untrussing.

(III.ii.110–12, 173)

If this be cynicism, it is far preferable to Angelo's puritanism, and is not wholly remote from the tolerance that the Duke's final judgements express; and a particularly incisive aspect of Lucio's sexual slanders is that they remind us that the Duke himself was responsible for that era of sexual licence which now he has appointed Angelo to curb. There is an ethically dubious quality about the Duke's devious procedures, and Lucio's bawdy allegations enable us, in the audience, to vent our distrust and retaliate against the Duke by our laughter.

That Lucio has acted as a cogently subversive force in the play is verified by the way in which the Duke, in the last scene, singles him out for final

117

and detailed attention. The threatened whipping and hanging is remitted, and a marriage – in prison – to the wronged Kate Keep-down is to be Lucio's punishment. 'Slandering a prince deserves it', says the Duke; but Lucio's real 'offence' has not been the mere slander of a prince. At their most insolently fanciful, Lucio's allegations have pointed towards ideological contradictions in the Duke's position and have challenged the basis of his paternalistic yet patently autocratic authority.

(iii)   Barnardine's Recalcitrance

Of the incursions which stage productions magnify, a vivid example is undoubtedly the incursion of Barnardine. He emerges late in the play (Act IV, scene iii), so his arrival is a theatrical surprise. He is angry, drunken, defiant, and a law to himself. Executioner, Pompey and Duke together can do nothing to move him to the block for death. His resistance stems from a form of Christian piety – the belief that only a sober person is in a state to make the act of contrition which should precede death – but in theatrical terms his presence is more subversive than this suggests. His sheer distinctive individuality challenges the principle that the law has the right to kill; and the brief alliance against him of the Friar-Duke, the ghoulish Abhorson and the immoral Pompey offers the sudden and visually stark suggestion that the power of the state depends on unsavoury and paradoxical alliances: even the brothel-world which appears to challenge it may validate and indirectly support the state's authority.

The brilliance of Shakespeare's imaginative realism is directly proportionate to his readiness to incorporate material which seems not to be strictly required by the evident plot and characterization. These incursionary elements not only give his dramas a quality of the unexpectedness and inconsequentiality of real life; they also introduce intelligent challenges to the ideology which the main narrative may seem to support; and in doing so they challenge, in principle, the bases of life's ideologies, which always seek to deny or tame the anomalous and unpredictable.

3.8   Various Critical Approaches

Given that a critic may change his mind, it may be an understatement to say that there are as many critical approaches as there are critics. Although it is customary and often reasonable to say that a particular approach is shared by a group of critics, the differences within that group may outweigh the similarities. There have been many Leavisites, but there was only one F. R. Leavis; there have been many ambiguity-hunters, but there was only one William Empson. The adoption of a given approach does not guarantee the merit of the result. A good critic may be Christian or agnostic, politically right-wing or left-wing; but his critical merit depends predominantly on his acumen, on his qualities of intelligence, sensitivity and imagination, and these qualities may be as well possessed by a Samuel Johnson as by a Jean-Paul Sartre. The approaches summarized in the following sections should be judged according to their fruitfulness rather than their 'correctness'.

3.81 *Christian and Anti-Christian*

In '*Measure for Measure* and the Gospels' (1930) G. Wilson Knight made a powerful counter-attack against one of the dominant orthodoxies concerning the play, the view that it was morbid and inwardly divided. Far from being divided, it was a splendid unity:

Much has been said about the difficulties of *Measure for Measure*. But, in truth, no play of Shakespeare shows more thoughtful care, more deliberate purpose, more consummate skill in structural technique, and, finally, more penetrating ethical and psychological insight. None shows a more exquisitely inwoven pattern.[21]

The basis of that pattern is 'the sublime strangeness and unreason of Jesus' teaching'; 'The play must be read ..... as a parable'; it 'tends towards allegory or symbolism'. 'Isabella stands for sainted purity, Angelo for Pharisaical righteousness, the Duke for a psychologically sound and enlightened ethic. Lucio represents indecent wit.' 'The Duke's sense of human responsibility is delightful throughout: he is like a kindly father, and all the rest are his children'; he is 'automatically comparable with Divinity'. Wilson Knight postulated many allusions to the Bible: the play's title refers to Matthew VII, the Duke's attitude to sexual sin is that of Jesus to the woman taken in adultery (John VIII), and the plot should remind us of the parables of the Prodigal Son (Luke XV) and the Unmerciful Servant (Matthew XVIII). A stern ethic is tested; human fallibility is revealed; and finally the Christian 'moral of love' is vindicated.

As we have seen, this challenging essay had a great influence on subsequent critics and directors of the play; notably on F. R. Leavis, Henri Fluchère, Roy Battenhouse and Nevill Coghill. In turn, it attracted a variety of counter-attacks, of which the most adroitly penetrating and theologically insolent was probably A. D. Nuttall's.[22] For him, the play is jagged and awkward: it displays technical neatness and metaphysical disorder; it resembles 'a minuet worked out in a sequence of violent discords'. We should recognize 'that Angelo is, on a modest computation . . . . . , worth about six Dukes'. It is Angelo's stern ethic which, in practice, we do and should support. The play offers a 'tender' Christian ethic: 'No man who is not himself perfect has the right to judge a fellow creature. Man can only forgive . . . . .' It also offers a related 'tender' but non-Christian ethic: 'anybody without a bit of generous vice in him isn't properly human'; like the former, this advises us to forgive. Against these, the play offers a 'tough' ethic: '*of course* none of us is perfect but *of course* we must judge':

> Now, do we really think that because none of us is perfect so no one should judge – that is, in hard terms, there should be no law-courts, no penal system, no juries, no police? Certainly judges are imperfect, but equally certainly it is a job that someone has to do. Men of tender conscience may preserve their charity intact, but only so long as others are willing to tarnish theirs a little.[23]

Angelo's ethic naturally lacks the tender ethic's power to 'give us warm feelings', but it is practical, it is supported by Shakespeare's presentation of the foul brothel-world, and it is ours.

Furthermore, commentators who see in the play a version of the Christian doctrine of the Atonement have failed (Nuttall claims) to draw an obvious conclusion. The closest counterpart to Christ is Angelo: 'Angelo is at once a Redeemer and the polluted'; he is a deputy, he bears sins, and he suffers. And if the Duke resembles God, this should fill us with misgivings about God: 'the Duke is both the Heavenly Father and supremely contemptible'. One precedent for his conduct is to be found in Machiavelli's account, in *The Prince*, of Cesare Borgia:

> the province was a prey to robbery, assaults, and every kind of disorder. He, therefore, judged it necessary to give them a good government in order to make them peaceful and obedient to his rule. For this purpose he appointed Messer Remirro de Orco, a cruel and able man, to whom he gave the fullest authority. This man, in a short time, was highly successful in rendering the country orderly and united, whereupon the duke, not deeming such excessive authority expedient, lest it should become hateful, appointed a civil court of justice in the centre of the province under an excellent president, to which each city appointed its own advocate. And as he knew that the harshness of the past had engendered some amount of hatred, in order to purge the minds of the people and to win them over completely, he resolved to show that if any cruelty had taken place it was not by his orders, but through the harsh disposition of his minister. And having found the

opportunity he had him cut in half and placed one morning in the public square at Cesena with a piece of wood and bloodstained knife at his side. The ferocity of this spectacle caused the people both satisfaction and amazement.[24]

Nuttall's criticisms of the Duke are these. First, he is ethically irresponsible. Having ruled so slackly that corruption is rife, he gives Angelo the task of reforming the state, instead of facing up to that responsibility himself; and when, as he wished, the laws are sternly enforced, 'he proceeds by his orgy of clemency at the close to undo all the good achieved'. The Duke is inconsistent in seeking simultaneously to test Angelo and to tighten the administration of Vienna by the most reliable means; if he has doubts about Angelo's probity, he should not entrust him with this important task. Furthermore, when in priestly disguise, the Duke displays 'unblushing readiness to hear confessions (and talk about them afterwards)'. Angelo commits vile acts, but 'the play gives him immense moral stature'; the Duke may be the hero, but 'he is utterly wanting in moral stature. Why else does Shakespeare repeatedly subject him to a kind of minor humiliation at the hands of the low persons of the play (see I I I.ii.89–92 and V.i.520–21)?'

Nuttall's essay, even in its atheistic zest, offers a completely symmetrical alternative to Wilson Knight's. The earlier critic was astute in drawing attention to the numerous Christian allusions of the play, but he exaggerated their co-ordinating significance. The characterization and the ethical problems are too complex to permit the work to be read as 'parable' or 'allegory', as he recommended, and he certainly sentimentalized the Duke. Nuttall's case is strongest when he defines the Duke's inconsistencies; it is less confident when he is acting as devil's, or Angelo's, advocate, and here he limits his account by terming it that of a 'substructure'. Nuttall says that the play offers the clash of theoretic absolutes (man must punish all, or forgive all) and offers only glimmerings of a *via media* in the person of Escalus. One objection to this is that Escalus's moderation is re-echoed by the Provost; another, and larger, objection is that what the Duke finally offers is not an 'orgy of clemency': Angelo has suffered an extreme of guilt and remorse, and must marry Mariana; Claudio has experienced guilt and terror; Lucio must make amends to Kate; and Barnardine has already languished long in jail and is provided with a counsellor. This exemplifies a procedure more judicious and selective than simple clemency. The Duke himself has learnt some important practical lessons; in future, justice may be maintained by a more vigilant and careful head of state, aided not only by Escalus but also by the Provost (who is to be employed 'in a worthier place'). It could be argued, then, that the basis has now been established for a government which, in its judicial procedures, is reasonably humane and selective but also practical: less radiantly merciful than Wilson Knight suggested, but less irresponsible than Nuttall alleged. Nevertheless, a view which the play does not make explicit but which, thanks to Claudio and Barnardine, is within its range of suggestion, is that government is too important to be entrusted to well-intentioned autocrats.

When Nevill Coghill, following Wilson Knight, introduced his own Christian interpretation of the play, he prefaced it with a satiric account of an imaginary, modish and, in his view, quite erroneous production. A modish producer, he suggested, might be guided by Dover Wilson and Clifford Leech, who have emphasized the work's cynicism.

He will discover in the Duke an unctuous fraud who abdicates his already neglected duties in order to play the unsavoury part of eavesdropper; a man who sneaks, under the guise of holiness, from one dark corner to another, smelling out other people's consciences. The producer will be careful to note what Lucio says of the Duke and will contrive in some of these dark corners a glimpse of him at grips with a mouthing beggar of fifty, and the ring of a ducat in a clack-dish.[25]

'This would be lofty,' remarked Coghill sardonically. 'But would it be Shakespearian?' His answer is an emphatic 'No'; our answer, surely, is 'It *could* be; indeed, you have made it so.' The imaginary production which Coghill evokes with mordant gusto may be distortive, but it has cogency; and his very sense of that dangerous element of cogency gives dialectical vigour to Coghill's own contrasting interpretation, according to which the play is a comedy in a radically pious sense, for it expresses the Christian doctrine of the fortunate fault: *'O felix culpa! O necessarium peccatum Adae!'*[26]

One of the characteristics of *Measure for Measure* is its readiness to dramatize contrasting extremes. If critics, in their egotism, ideological prejudices and love of Shakespeare, themselves emphasize now one extreme and now another, that process, too, may in the eyes of their considerate reader amount to a fortunate fault.

3.82 Structuralist and Post-Structuralist

Structuralism became influential in the 1960s and 1970s, and like various other '-isms' and some '-ologies' it purported to bring a new rigour and objectivity to the study of cultural entities. It was strongly influenced by an apparently self-contradictory notion attributed to Saussure: 'Concepts are purely differential and defined not by their positive content but negatively by their relations with the other terms of the system.'[27] This notion held some ambiguity: do concepts have positive content or not? Popularizers generally took it to mean that they did not, which rendered the notion self-contradictory: for if concepts had no content other than the relational, they would contain nothing to relate. Nevertheless, structuralists obediently endeavoured to examine numerous chosen entities not in terms of feelings or moral values or information about the world but in terms of postulated structures of internal relationships. Structures of binary opposition became the most popular, since these offered the simplest way of accommodating a variety of differences. Beside Saussure, another potent influence was Freud, whose dream-analyses postulated remarkable contrasts between manifest and latent significances: it seemed that an analyst skilled in modes of displacement, substitution, condensation and symbolism could infer from the apparent story a deeper and truer story.

A particularly important practical demonstration of structuralism was Claude Lévi-Strauss's analysis of the Oedipus myth.[28] Lévi-Strauss selected what he deemed to be the most important elements of the myth and arranged them in four columns of a chart or table. Thus 'Oedipus marries his mother', and similar elements, entered column 1; 'Oedipus kills his father' entered column 2; 'Oedipus kills the Sphinx' entered column 3; and 'Oedipus = *swollen foot (?)*' entered column 4. Items in the first column, he explained, illustrated 'the overrating of blood relations'; those in the second, 'underrating of blood relations'; in the third, 'denial of the autochthonous [i.e. earth-born] nature of man'; and in the fourth, 'persistence of the autochthonous origin of man'. This quaternary pattern could then yield a binary opposition: 'The overrating of blood relations is to the underrating of blood relations as the attempt to escape autochthony is to the impossibility to succeed in it.'[29] The meaning of the whole myth was thus a contradiction: people believed that human beings were born from the earth, yet they also knew that human beings were born from women. Lévi-Strauss's notion of the symmetrical structure of the myth resembled the 'thematic four-term homology' (derived from J. A. Greimas) commended by David Lodge. This assumes that fictional narratives are the elaboration of a four-term pattern: A is to B as not-A is to not-B (e.g. Life is to Death as Non-Life is to Non-Death).[30]

Lévi-Strauss's method is open to various objections. One is that different commentators will disagree about what the important elements of a myth or narrative are, and will therefore postulate conflicting 'deep structures'; and this, in turn, will call in question the objective existence of any postulated 'deep structure'. Another criticism is that the resultant diagram does little to explain the varying vitality of the myth or story in its various embodiments: even if the structuralist's X-ray reveals the true skeleton, our attraction is to the living body rather than to white bones beneath. Indeed, adopting the four-term pattern, we could offer a structural diagram of the analogy between a structuralist analysis and an X-ray picture of the body:

1 structural scheme	2 perceived skeleton
whole text 3	living body 4

Thus 1 resembles 2 as 3 resembles 4, and 1 differs from 3 as 2 differs from 4. The structuralist's X-ray can, of course, be helpful in two contrasting ways. A picture of the skeleton may help us to understand the living body, and the repellent starkness of the bones may give us a renewed appreciation of the pulsing warmth of the living person.

Among Shakespeare's comedies, it is the late works, *Pericles, Cymbeline, The Winter's Tale* and *The Tempest*, which most hospitably beckon the structuralist, for in them we sense a marked tension between the narrative surface, with its intricacies and realistic detail, and a simpler but more resonant mythic sub-structure. '[W]ith the disappearance and revival of Hermione in *The Winter's Tale*', says Northrop Frye, 'the original nature-myth of Demeter and Proserpine is openly established';[31] and this nature-myth is related to those of Orpheus and Eurydice and of Admetus and Alcestis. *Measure for Measure* is urban, contemporaneous and realistic, rather than pastoral, archaic and mythic; but one could, with a stretch of the imagination, see as its elemental structure that ritual proclaimed by Sir James Frazer which, for Frye, is the origin of both tragedy and comedy: 'This is the ritual of the struggle, death and rebirth of a God-Man, which is linked to the yearly triumph of spring over winter'. (After the descent into the region of death, and the dispatch of a corpse, Ragozine, to redeem Claudio, the Duke emerges with stronger power and inaugurates the procreative festivities of new marriage.) Now this theory might tell us something of interest about the play's aetiology, its remote pre-Christian ancestry, but it tells us little about the distinctiveness of the play itself. The same may be an objection to another kind of 'deep structure' postulated by Frye: a Freudian pattern. Discussing classical 'New Comedy', Frye says that it 'unfolds from what may be described as a comic Oedipus situation':

Its main theme is the successful effort of a young man to outwit an opponent and possess the girl of his choice. The opponent is usually the father (*senex*) . . . . . The father frequently wants the same girl, and is cheated out of her by the son . . . . . [I]t turns out that she is not under an insuperable taboo after all but is an accessible object of desire, so that the plot follows the regular wish-fulfilment pattern. Often the central Oedipus situation is thinly concealed by surrogates or doubles of the main characters . . . . .[32]

Parts of *Measure for Measure* do indeed seem to shift and re-align themselves in response to this Oedipal scheme. In the play, the *senex* or father-figure, the Duke, who had sought to curb sexuality in the state, does eventually propose marriage to his protégée, the youthful Isabella. The 'taboo' (her novitiate as a nun) seems to be dispelled. There has indeed been an arrangement of 'surrogates or doubles'. The Duke's authority was given to Angelo, who sought by coercive power to take Isabella's virginity; but she was saved by another surrogate, Mariana. It is not a young lover of Isabella who is threatened with decapitation ('Decapitation is to us a well-known symbolic substitute for castration,' says Freud),[33] but her brother; yet his sexual desires have led her into the sexual peril imposed by authority. A Freudian could readily see the play as a drama of sexual rebellion by the young against paternal authority: authority counter-attacks repressively; guilt is generated on both sides; and, by means of a division of roles, a social compromise can eventually be attained.

One does not need to be a Freudian, however, to see the neatly ironic structure provided by the theme of substitution. It can be summed up in tabular form:

Destructive Substitution	*Constructive Substitution*
Angelo deputizes for the Duke.	The Duke supersedes Angelo.
A maidenhead (Isabella's) is required instead of a head (Claudio's).	A maidenhead (Mariana's) is substituted for Isabella's.
Angelo's warrant confirming the execution is sent instead of the promised reprieve.	The Duke's warrant (ensuring Claudio's reprieve) supersedes Angelo's.
Barnardine's head is to be substituted for Claudio's.	Ragozine's head is substituted for Claudio's.

An alternative table, which again may serve as an indicator or mnemonic of some of the play's ironies and correlations, is suggested by the theme of restraint. It could be claimed that the play offers a broad contrast between 'liberating restraint' and 'wasteful confinement'. One liberating restraint is marriage as a basis of the family; another is considerate justice as a basis of the state; and the play's ending suggests that the two should go together. One kind of wasteful confinement is the brothel, where women are degraded and the seeds of life are dispersed; another kind is the prison, where living beings are 'buried alive' and may be executed. Shakespeare links the latter pair adroitly by showing the partnership in prison of the executioner Abhorson ('abhorrent whore's-son') and the procurer, Pompey. The Provost says that they weigh equally: 'a feather will turn the scale'; and Pompey remarks: 'I am as well acquainted here as I was in our house of profession: one would think it were Mistress Overdone's own house, for here be many of her old customers.'[34] The structural table might resemble that on page 127.

There 1 resembles 2 as 3 resembles 4, and 1 contrasts with 3 as 2 contrasts with 4. Just as the alliance of Abhorson with Pompey suggests that Shakespeare intends us to see resemblances between the world of the prison and the world of the brothel, so the Duke's proposal of marriage to Isabella as he completes his restoration of considerate justice suggests that Shakespeare intends us to relate the political to the familial and to see analogies between the harmonious state and the loving family. The contrast between 1 and 3 is not total: justice in the state, however 'considerate', entails the maintenance of prisons; and the contrast between 2 and 4 is not total, because Mistress Overdone has acted as a foster-mother. The play intermittently brings to mind William Blake's aphorism: 'Prisons are built with stones of Law, Brothels with bricks of Religion.'[35]

We see, therefore, that a 'structuralist' approach to a play like this may

Liberating Restraint	*Wasteful Confinement*
1	3
considerate justice (harmonious social life)	prison and execution (wasted social life)
Duke + Isabella	Abhorson + Pompey
love and mariage (familial life)	brothel and prostitution (wasted life)
2	4

postulate a 'deep' structure, in which case there may be a large disparity between the apparent import of the work and its postulated underlying import; or it may postulate a 'shallow' structure, which is closer to the apparent import of the work but remains starkly schematic. It may graphically expose some thematic linkages and ironies. Its concern with tabular clarities and binary oppositions can lead to ludicrous over-simplifications, and it cannot discriminate between a third-rate work and a first-rate one.

Hostility to structuralism's 'tabular clarities and binary oppositions' was part of the impetus of post-structuralism and deconstructionism. Adherents of these related persuasions were fond of radical paradoxes and apparent self-contradictions within texts; and they were particularly pleased by works which seemed to be about themselves rather than about the world: self-referential, self-subverting texts were eagerly sought (and language itself was sometimes deemed to be merely self-referential and self-subverting). They listened hard for silences or reticences in a work, deeming these to be evidence of an impasse generated by contradiction. As textual contradictions might be the product of ideological conflict in society, there was some overlap between deconstructionism and Marxism;[36] but at its most extreme, in its denial that language relates to anything beyond itself, deconstructionism was self-defeating and 'utterly conservative'.[37] In its milder and more practical forms, it differed little in basic principle from the procedures of past critics like D. H. Lawrence, William Empson or, for that matter, Basil Willey, who had given close attention to tensions and contradictions within the works they examined.

As no text can discuss everything, it is not a matter of great difficulty to discover that a text is replete with silences and reticences. Just as structuralists disagree in their identification of the significant elements which are to form the postulated structure, so deconstructionists disagree in their identification of the significant gaps. In *Measure for Measure*, as we have seen, a popular choice is likely to be the silence of Isabella when the Duke proposes marriage. One could argue that assent would demean her fiercely ascetic independence, so strongly established early in the play, while dissent would contradict her recent acquiescence in the Duke's benign authority; either way she has to sacrifice half her nature. Her silence places a question-mark against the autocratic ideology that the Duke embodies. Alternatively, one might point to the conspicuous absence of any kind of productive labour in this fictional Vienna. The populace is devoted to dissolute leisure, brothel-organizing, or to service of the state's administrative and penal system. Given that carpenters, weavers, shepherds and the like tend to figure as buffoons or simpletons in Shakespearian comedy, it may be felt that this absence is no great political loss; and if we grumbled at every text which, while portraying society with some realism, declined to indicate that a ruling elite depends for its wealth and power on the labours of the many, we would be repetitively grumbling at the vast majority of quasi-realistic texts between ancient times and the present. It will be said that we should make allowances for the likelihood that to Shakespeare, as to virtually everyone else in his society, the steeply hierarchical nature of its class-structure was regarded as natural and proper. Yet we may recall what Arnold Kettle once remarked about Jane Austen and her novel *Emma*:

The very concept of 'making allowances' of this sort for an artist is both insulting and mechanical. It has something of the puritan's contempt for those who have not seen the light, but it lacks the puritan's moral courage, for it is accompanied by a determination not to be done out of what cannot be approved . . . . .

The truth is that in so far as *Emma* does reveal her as a conventional member of her class, blindly accepting its position and ideology, the value of *Emma* is indeed limited, not just relatively, but objectively and always.[38]

Whether a similarly stern political judgement is applicable to Shakespeare is a question pursued by some of the critics who are cited in the following pages. We may note here that 'deconstructionism', in its concern with politically significant contradictions and omissions, often entailed distrust of traditional classics of literature. Shakespeare's plays, and other famous literary works, have sometimes been termed 'canonical texts' by critics who wish to suggest that such texts have been given prominence by a cultural establishment which senses that they will exert a predominantly conservative influence. This suggestion has been challenged on various grounds. In a left-wing magazine, Kiernan Ryan said that

> if the works in question . . . . . always and inevitably prove 'reactionary' when read, then the relentless investment of critical energy in their conservative interpretation since the Renaissance would have been ludicrously superfluous. There would scarcely be any point in repeatedly demonstrating the orthodox vision of a play, novel or poem whose endorsement of the ideological norms of its time was anyway self-evident and indisputable.

In short:

> It is surely possible (and, in my opinion, much more plausible) to maintain that it is precisely the subversive potential of certain literary works which has necessitated the endless institutionalized process . . . . .[39]

3.83 *Left-Wing and Feminist Approaches*

If a critic regards a text as valuable, egotism (and, no doubt, higher motives) will tempt him or her to offer an interpretation which implies that the text has astutely succeeded in adopting his or her own prejudices (or principles). Just as a Christian commentator is likely to emphasize the Christian elements of *Measure for Measure* and as a sceptical commentator is likely to emphasize its impious elements, so a politically right-wing critic is likely to commend conservative aspects of the text (e.g. by applauding the wisdom of the Duke) and a politically left-wing critic is likely to commend rebellious aspects (e.g. by paying sympathetic attention to Lucio and Pompey). Similarly, feminists may, understandably, magnify the importance and merit of Isabella, and may detect a complicity with Angelo in male critics who deem her neurotic.

As the Church and the State have sometimes tended to form an ideological alliance, jointly seeking to regulate sexual as well as overtly political life, radical thinkers have frequently given hospitality to the idea that the sexual liberation of the many may also herald their political liberation. William Blake and D. H. Lawrence expressed this idea powerfully and enduringly, and numerous lesser writers have entertained it; in the 1960s, for example, Herbert Marcuse's *Eros and Civilization* was, for a while, very influential among young left-wingers. Marcuse suggested that 'sexuality can, under specific conditions, create highly civilized human relations without being subjected to the repressive organization which the established civilization has imposed upon the instinct';[40] and he later summarized his idea thus:

'Polymorphous sexuality' was the term which I used to indicate that the new direction of progress would depend completely on the opportunity to activate repressed or arrested *organic*, biological needs: to make the human body the instrument of pleasure rather than labor.[41]

In literary theory, a partly related development was Mikhail Bakhtin's theory of the 'carnivalesque'.[42] He suggested that one radical, incursionary mode of resistance to established authority has long been the element of saturnalia, bacchanalia and festive misrule in society and in literature; and he relished the apparently subversive bawdry and irreverence in both Rabelais and Shakespeare, for they kept alive 'the utopian world'. Although Pompey Bum would be flattered by this theory, it could be objected, of course, that saturnalia and ceremonies of misrule (for example, those which took place in ancient Rome, sixteenth-century Paris and Elizabethan England) were permitted by authority as safety-valves for anarchic feelings, so that authority was actually strengthened by them. As Michel Foucault[43] and others have pointed out, the 'sexual revolution' which occurred in Western societies between 1950 and 1970 may have liberalized sexual attitudes but it left the main power-structures of society unchanged.

In 1983 Alan Sinfield (writing from a socialist standpoint) suggested that in *Measure for Measure* the principal challenge to authority stems not from the licence of the brothel-world but from the desire of young people freely to choose their partners in marriage. The play addresses a tension between this desire and paternal authority.

By stressing mutual affection and male domination in marriage protestantism set up a tension. It proved fatal in paradise and must have been difficult for many in the seventeenth century.
The other disjunction in the Reformation doctrine of marriage occurred because theorists wanted to maintain, as well as the husband's authority, the father's . . . . . The ideal of affectionate marriage was held alongside a continuing belief in parental control, mainly in the interests of social standing and financial security.[44]

In the play, Juliet may eventually be happily reunited with Claudio, but

Angelo is compelled to wed Mariana: 'Look that you love your wife,' the Duke tells him (V.i.495). Should we assume, with the handbooks, that affection will develop in time; or will they be obliged, in Milton's words, 'spite of antipathy, to fadge together'? (*Complete Prose*, II, 236). The further instance of Lucio and his punk suggests the latter. And does Isabella love the Duke and could she, if she wished, refuse his proposal? . . . . .

The elegant pairing off which concludes relatively untroubled comedies occurs here in circumstances which imply its hollowness. Whereas in earlier plays Shakespeare was happy to indulge in genial adjustments to secure the coincidence of love and social approval, in *Measure for Measure* he allows us to perceive that the celebratory betrothal procession may mask an uneasy compromise, an instrument of social control. We are left to envisage for ourselves a more humane way of organizing society.[45]

The claim that *Measure for Measure* offers an object-lesson in suspect modes of social control was further extended, a year or two later, by Jonathan Dollimore.[46] He said:

Via the Duke's personal intervention and integrity, authoritarian reaction is put into abeyance but not discredited: the corrupt deputy is unmasked but no law is repealed, and the mercy exercised remains the prerogative of the same ruler who initiated reaction . . . . .

The transgressors in *Measure for Measure* signify neither the unregeneracy of the flesh, nor the ludic subversive carnivalesque. Rather, through them the spectre of unregulated desire legitimates an exercise in authoritarian repression. And of course it is a spectre: desire is never unregulated, least of all in Jacobean London . . . . .

What Foucault has said of sexuality in the nineteenth and twentieth centuries seems appropriate also to sexuality as a sub-category of sin in earlier periods: it *appears* to be that which power is afraid of but in actuality is that which power works through. Sin, especially when internalized as guilt, has produced the subjects of authority as surely as any ideology . . . . .

Even those who appear to offer resistance to authority actually endorse it. Pompey readily serves as hangman's assistant; Lucio struts and postures as a loyal foe to subversion when supporting Angelo and Escalus against the 'friar'. Furthermore, 'the prostitutes, the most exploited group in the society which the play represents, are absent from it':

Virtually everything that happens presupposes them yet they have no voice, no presence. And those who speak for them do so as exploitatively as those who want to eliminate them.

It appears that one theme of the discussions by Sinfield and Dollimore has its keynote in Elbow's repeated confusion of 'respected' and 'suspected' (II.i. 159–75): the respected Duke is now suspected, and the text is valued not for the ducal process which Wilson Knight, Leavis and Coghill found so humane, but for its illustrations of the devious ways by

131

which authority controls and represses humanity. We may recall that between 1931 and 1934 Bertolt Brecht converted *Measure for Measure* into *Die Rundköpfe und die Spitzköpfe* (*Round Heads and Pointed Heads*), a Marxist allegory in which the Duke becomes a Viceroy who represents capitalism, while Angelo becomes Angelo Iberin, a deputy who represents Adolf Hitler. At a time of economic discontent, Iberin foments hostility between two arbitrarily denominated social groups: the round heads and the pointed heads. Eventually, the returning Viceroy resumes power and pardons everyone except a group of revolutionaries (their emblem is the sickle), who are sentenced to death. Brecht thus suggests that the capitalists have employed Hitler to foment anti-semitism in order to distract people's attention from economic exploitation. Brecht's allegory was criticized by subsequent history: by the Molotov–Ribbentrop pact of 1939 and by the alliance of Stalin, Roosevelt and Churchill against Hitler (in a war during which Brecht chose to reside not in the U.S.S.R. but in sunny California).

Apart from the requirement to indicate approval of Marx and of social revolution which liberates the workers, there is little agreement about what should constitute a Marxist approach to literature. Critics who deem themselves to be Marxists have adopted conflicting approaches (formalism, socialist realism, structuralism, post-structuralism, etc.) and have been assailed by other critics who purport to be Marxists. It is notable that Karl Marx and Friedrich Engels, in their enthusiasm for Balzac, made clear that the merit of a writer does not depend on his holding a left-wing position.[47] Among feminists, too, there is considerable diversity and conflict. Normally, a feminist approach to Shakespeare gives special attention to the female characters and searches the text for further evidence that women have long been exploited by men but have displayed a capacity for resistance.

In *Shakespeare and the Nature of Women* (1975), Juliet Dusinberre claimed that Shakespeare transcended masculine prejudice and aided the cause of women by popularizing the Protestant reformers' hostility to monasticism and their advocacy of the married state. Thus, in *Measure for Measure*, Isabella learns that the true testing-ground for virtue is the world of practical endeavour and eventual marriage rather than the maidenly seclusion of the cloister. Predominantly, his works prove that

Shakespeare saw men and women as equal in a world which declared them unequal. He did not divide human nature into the masculine and the feminine, but observed in the individual woman or man an infinite variety of union between opposing impulses.[48]

132

Later, the critic Anne Barton made, in more polemical style, a similar claim for Shakespeare:

No other writer challenges the aggressively limited feminist position, the intolerant and rigidly schematized view of human life . . . . . with such power. At the same time, disconcertingly, no other writer has created as many memorable and sensitively understood women characters.[49]

Marilyn French, in *Shakespeare's Division of Experience* (1982), argued that though Shakespeare experienced a pathological 'horror of sex' he also recognized that males needed to value and absorb 'inlaw feminine qualities': 'nutritiveness, compassion, mercy'. When Isabel pleads for Angelo, she is pleading for 'mercy for human sexuality itself':

Allowing herself also sexual [*sic*], despite her renunciation, she admits that even a 'saint' has a bond with the rest of humankind, that all humans feel desire. She thereby pleads the case of humankind in a tribunal that is trying sex . . . . . In a division of experience along gender lines, and an attribution of dominance to one pole, sex is necessarily sinful. But since all humans are sexual, even the most chaste and constant nun, we must forgive ourselves and each other, and leave it to heaven to punish this 'sin'.[50]

The reader may think this a rather hyperbolic gloss on the speech in which Isabella defends Angelo by saying that it was just to execute Claudio for copulating with Juliet. Marilyn French's book also indicates a much larger problem. If a feminist work proceeds from the assumption of a basic contrast between a feminine nature (e.g. nutritive and altruistic) and a masculine nature (e.g. aggressive and egoistic), then it appears to reconstitute the limiting and divisive stereotypes which elsewhere feminism questions. If, on the other hand, it consistently opposes the cultural allocation of distinctive natures to the masculine and feminine, its basic model may therefore be that of an open, androgynous self, so that the approach may become no more feminist than masculist. (To liberate women from their stereotypes would entail liberating men from the complementary stereotypes.)

Marilyn French's 'division of experience' was criticized by Lisa Jardine in *Still Harping on Daughters* (1983), which gave particular attention to the matter of stereotyping. Jardine claimed that Shakespeare's female characters, for all their apparent diversity, can almost always be related to a range of stereotypes which help to maintain masculine dominance. One such stereotype is the 'patient Griselda': the woman who is quiet, patient and submissive, even when subjected to harsh and cruel treatment by her husband; another is the 'Lucretia', the ravished virgin who subsequently kills herself. The latter category is represented not only by

Lucrece, of course, in 'The Rape of Lucrece', but also by Lavinia in *Titus Andronicus*; while the 'print of Griselda' is to be found, Jardine says, on Julia (*Two Gentlemen of Verona*), Hero (*Much Ado About Nothing*), Viola (*Twelfth Night*), Helena (*All's Well That Ends Well*), Desdemona (*Othello*), Imogen (*Cymbeline*), Marina (*Pericles*) and Hermione (*The Winter's Tale*). Another category is that of the martyred female saint. In *Measure for Measure*, however, Isabella does seem to defy the stereotypes – but then they take revenge on her by making the audience feel hostile to a heroine who does not comply with their traditional models of submissiveness.

[T]he expectations concerning saintly virgins whose virtue is assaulted are used to undermine Isabella's position during the crucial scenes in which she allows her brother to go to his death, rather than submit to Angelo.

Were Isabella Lucretia (and the similarities between the preliminary circumstances are extremely close in the two stories), she would submit to enforced sex, tell all afterwards, and kill herself. That is what the patriarchy expects of a female hero under such circumstances . . . . .

Were Isabella a female saint of *The Golden Legend* . . . . . she would flee in disguise and do interminable servile penance for the lust she has aroused . . . . .

Shakespeare's Isabella is belittled by the stereotypes to whom she so flagrantly refuses to match up. Her stature is diminished, her virtue is placed in question . . . . . Isabella's crude accusation of 'incest', and the claim that her enforced sex would 'make a man' of Claudio does nothing to elevate her in the audience's eyes. Indeed, it suggests curiously that Isabella is accusing *Claudio* of wanting to rape her, betraying an obsessive fear of her own sexuality in general.[51]

French's argument gives the impression, then, that whatever Shakespeare's heroines do, they are perpetuating the demeaning stereotypes. If the heroines match them, they propagate them; and if (as in the exceptional case of Isabella) they do not match them, the stereotypes and the audience will belittle the heroines.

Originally, the noun 'stereotype' meant 'a solid metallic plate for printing': it could produce numerous identical prints. In literature and in life, both men and woman can be classified according to types: the professional soldier, the dedicated nurse, the astute businessman, the militant feminist, the devoted father, and so forth. Frequently these afford conveniently brief descriptive categories: we might rapidly describe a new acquaintance by relating him or her to several of them. But, by definition, no two individuals are identical. Comparison with the type may be a way of defining a person's distinctive individuality: to compare is to contrast. In a third-rate play, characters may too predictably conform to traditional types; or, alternatively, its characterization may seem implausibly and inconsistently free, giving an impression of incoherence. Shakespeare's Hotspur, Hector, Antony and Coriolanus all belong to the type of the brave yet rash warrior, but each is distinct from the others, having unique and plausible individuation. If some of Shakespeare's self-willed women meet tragic fates, so do some of his self-willed men; and if the heroines of his comedies seem predictably destined for marriage rather than for independent careers, such was life for most young women in his day. An important consideration is the direction of Shakespeare's innovations in characterization. In his most fully drawn characters, both male and female alike are endowed with unprecedented powers of articulate intelligence, with mercurial linguistic energies to fuse the private and the public, the abstract and the concrete, the particular and the general. Such extraordinary articulacy may flatter ordinary humankind, or it may celebrate through local realization a vast unrealized potential. Shakespeare extends the capacity for individual experience by liberating, and letting us share, new territories of defined experience. In such territories, the explorations of Cleopatra, Perdita and Isabella are no less important than those of Antony, Florizel and Claudio.

Part 4   Conclusion

How the Text Criticizes Its Critics

The text of *Measure for Measure* moves through time and space, waning in prestige when the cultural phase is uncongenial, waxing in prestige as conditions change. Countless thousands of people have lent part of their life-energies to it: actors, directors, scholars, critics, translators, teachers, pupils, students. There is no foreseeable end to the process of scholarly exegesis, not only because every year brings to light some new source or analogue, but also because each passing year renders some familiar phrase or reference less familiar and proportionately in need of explanation. Similarly, there is no foreseeable end to the process of critical evaluation, because, as society changes, critics will repeatedly seek to relate the text to new preoccupations and problems. What is evident is that, at present, *Measure for Measure* enjoys greater critical respect and theatrical interest than ever before. It has triumphed over those critics who once regarded it with scorn and revulsion.

If intelligence is indeed the art of relevance-making, of establishing connections between apparently unconnected things, then *Measure for Measure* abundantly demonstrates this intelligence; and we as readers may vicariously experience such Shakespearian intelligence, enjoy its results and intermittently learn it. This connection-making facility is evident whether we consider the texture of the language, the range of characterization or the thematic interaction of the varied scenes. At the same time, there is something to tantalize us as well as to gratify us: we sense occasional textual enigmas, minor inconsistencies in plotting, possible lacunae in its dramatized debates, and the apparent decline in tone and texture as the Friar-Duke advances his schemes. A critical account may refine or adulterate our response.

When we take an admirable critical essay on *Measure for Measure* and compare it with our experience of the work, we will see obvious differences. The essay selects certain features and organizes them as part of an explanatory argument. Even if the features which are omitted do not seem to invalidate the argument, they will haunt it as the potential of alternative emphases and thus alternative arguments. The explanatory endeavour may augment both understanding and, eventually, pleasure; but the critical discourse of rational prose is mocked by the varied discourses of dramatic poetry and speech, with their intense co-ordination of the rational, the instinctual and the emotional. The play may be a 'criticism of life', yet, simultaneously, it is holiday; and the interpretation which does not trivialize may, instead, solemnize: so that part of the text will jeer and snigger at it. The admirable essay may seem to provide plenty of answers and give the certitudes of hindsight, but the pleasure of the drama lay largely in our experience of tentative multiple foresight – our attempt to grasp major questions and imagine alternative answers. The pleasure lay also in our sense that the story was generating numerous potential stories as it progressed towards a dénouement which eventually defined a major sequence and simultaneously exorcized those other, alternative sequences which had existed as possibilities. Will Claudio live or die? If he survives, how? And what will the consequences be for Isabella? What is Angelo really like? How will he be outwitted? What kind of justice does he deserve, and what will he get? How will he respond to it? Criticism tends to deal with the realized plot-sequence; but the imagination was generating numerous plot-sequences, the unrealized ones too; and it was our partisan interest in one or two of them, an allegiance kept vigilant by the inferred presence of the alternatives, that generated our imaginative suspense. Art is long and life is short, so the critics' concentration on the realized *Measure for Measure* is understandable; but all those unrealized alternative plays were, for a while, a real part of our responsive experience.

During the play, our ethical judgements have been sometimes supported and sometimes contradicted by our aesthetic judgements: an argument of which we disapprove ethically may have been expressed in ways that are aesthetically pleasing. Our moral hopes have sometimes been opposed by our love of imaginative excitement: we hope that Claudio will not be executed, but part of us relishes the prospect of the dramatic turmoil that would ensue if he were. Even though we may already be thoroughly familiar with the outcome, a good stage production will not only renew our attention to the immediate but will also thereby regenerate our sense of alternative predictive sequences. We may experience a marked contrast between the play as constructed by our reading of the text and the play constructed before us on stage. And we recognize that no production of it will be 'neutral'. The settings, the tone and style of the Duke, the modes of interaction of the characters generally, may emphasize right-wing rather than left-wing political implications, or sceptical rather than religious commendations.

In the body of this book, my own prejudices and my misgivings about parts of *Measure for Measure* will have been evident; but when I pause for further reflection and again turn over the pages of the text, the glories of its intense articulacy revive my humility, and its bold explorations of new territories of defined experience make the prosaic discourse of even radical commentators seem timidly conservative. The strife of wills and intelligences between Isabella and Angelo; the contrasting meditations on death by the Duke and Claudio; the cheeky cogency of Pompey and the dogged defiance by Barnardine; the crystalline lyricism of the Boy's song; the newly memorable statements of the familiar, and the incessant questing into the unfamiliar: all these at once mock, challenge and exhort the commentator. Accordingly, I shall conclude with two reminders of the text's diversities.

Here is Angelo, replying to Escalus in Act II, scene i:

> *'Tis one thing to be tempted, Escalus,*
> *Another thing to fall. I not deny*
> *The jury passing on the prisoner's life*
> *May in the sworn twelve have a thief, or two,*
> *Guiltier than him they try. What's open made to justice,*
> *That justice seizes. What knows the laws*
> *That thieves do pass on thieves? 'Tis very pregnant,*
> *The jewel that we find, we stoop and take 't,*
> *Because we see it; but what we do not see,*
> *We tread upon, and never think of it.*
> *You may not so extenuate his offence*
> *For I have had such faults; but rather tell me,*
> *When I that censure him do so offend,*
> *Let mine own judgement pattern out my death,*
> *And nothing come in partial. Sir, he must die.*

Angelo is coolly, logically, defending his view that the law must be firmly implemented and that fallibility in the judge is not a valid reason for showing mercy to Claudio. He is rational but characteristically inflexible; he seems already to have forgotten the Duke's edict that both 'Mortality and mercy' should live in his tongue and heart. Angelo's judicious rationality forms part of a pattern of contrasts: it sets in sharp relief the later fervour of Isabella, the anguish of Claudio, and the confusion under temptation of Angelo himself. And there is strong proleptic irony: the man who here says, 'When I that censure him do so offend,/Let mine own judgement pattern out my death', will indeed be reduced to seeking 'Immediate sentence, then, and sequent death'.

His reasoning is lucid and concise, moving rapidly between the particular problem and the general observation. The speech is 'in character', and for a particular dramatic occasion; yet it gives lapidary definition to common experience, new terse memorability to familiar knowledge: 'What's open made to justice, that justice seizes'; 'The jewel that we find, we stoop and take 't,/Because we see it; but what we do not see,/We tread upon, and never think of it'. What makes commentators talk of the 'universality' of Shakespeare is not just a matter of the range of characterization and emotion; it is largely a matter of Shakespeare's mercurial facility in moving from a particular fictional situation into a mass of familiar experience and giving that experience new, memorable and enduring formulation: he generates the sense that any experience is potentially definable and valuable.

The second example is taken from Pompey's self-defence at the court case in Act II, scene i.

POMPEY   *And I beseech you, look into Master Froth here, sir; a man of fourscore pound a year; whose father died at Hallowmas – was't not at Hallowmas, Master Froth?*

FROTH   *All-hallond Eve.*

POMPEY   *Why, very well: I hope here be truths. He, sir, sitting, as I say, in a lower chair, sir – 'twas in the Bunch of Grapes, where indeed you have a delight to sit, have you not?*

FROTH   *I have so, because it is an open room, and good for winter . . . . .*

Later:

ESCALUS   *. . . . . the law will not allow it, Pompey; nor it shall not be allowed in Vienna.*

POMPEY   *Does your worship mean to geld and splay all the youth of the city?*

ESCALUS   *No, Pompey.*

POMPEY   *Truly, sir, in my poor opinion, they will to't then. If your worship will take order for the drabs and the knaves, you need not to fear the bawds,*

In the first part of this passage, Pompey is astutely conducting a defence by obfuscation: by deliberate digressions he is attempting to cloud the issue and weary the magistrates. Angelo soon departs impatiently, and Pompey will proceed to baffle Elbow and win a lenient caution for Froth and himself. Previously, as we have seen, Angelo had coolly and efficiently decided the fate of Claudio; now Pompey, the procurer, whose offence is, in principle, far graver than that of Claudio, will literally make a mockery of the law. The scene offers obvious comic relief and a relaxation of mode: after lucid and taut blank verse, we relax into colloquial prose and broad farce; but the ironies are serious and searching. Pompey's mode of address may seem obsequious ('I beseech you . . . . . sir . . . . sir . . . . sir') but his character is confident, cocky, cheeky. In the text and in the commentaries, sober moral judgements tend to wilt before such independent vitality.

Against the law's order, Pompey marshals society's muddle. Furthermore, his digressions are cogent in a Shakespearian sense and not only because they suit Pompey's purposes. Consider the business of Froth's sitting in a chair in the Bunch of Grapes on 'All-hallond Eve' ('because it is an open room, and good for winter'): these details rapidly give biographical substance and character to the peripheral Master Froth; as unpredictable details, apparently irrelevant to predictable narrative demands, they give three-dimensional substance and credibility to the fictional city; and since these vernacular references imply the English calendar and the familiar English tavern-world, they extend the imaginative location from Vienna to Britain, reminding us that in Shakespearian drama it is the comic characters who hold the magical pilot's licence to fly through space and time. And in the second part of the quoted passage, Pompey shows that he also holds the shrewd comedian's licence to thrust an astringently mundane common sense at the pomposities and legalities of authority: 'Does your worship mean to geld and splay all the youth of the city?' The firmness of Escalus, the moral sonorities of the Duke and even the fervour of Isabella – none of these is left wholly unscathed by the mundane mockery in that vivid question.

When the critics and commentators have completed their explanatory work, we are left with the stubbornly simple fact that, in most of his literary work, Shakespeare was more articulately intelligent, sensitive and imaginative than the vast majority of people; but those qualities have been transmitted to us, and, by means of texts like *Measure for Measure*, we can enjoy them, vicariously possess them, and extend them. We may add another chapter to 'a tale whose telling can never be finished'.

Part 5 Caudal

5.1 Notes

Part 1

1. See Richmond Noble: *Shakespeare's Biblical Knowledge* (London: S.P.C.K., 1935), pp. 75–6.
2. Such a view has been expressed by Georg Brandes in *William Shakespeare* (1898), John Dover Wilson in *The Essential Shakespeare* (1932), Una Ellis-Fermor in *The Jacobean Drama* (1936), Theodore Spencer in *Shakespeare and the Nature of Man* (1942), and by others.
3. Preface to *Plays Unpleasant* [1898] (Harmondsworth: Penguin, 1946), p. 22.

Part 2

1. 'To the Memory of My Beloued, the Avthor Mr. William Shakespeare: and What He Hath Left Vs', line 31. *William Shakespeare: The Complete Works*, ed. Peter Alexander (London and Glasgow: Collins, 1951), p. xxviii.
2. *Groats-Worth of Witte* (Edinburgh University Press, 1966), p. 45.
3. Thomas Dekker: *The Gull's Horn-Book* [1609], ed. R. B. McKerrow (London: De la More Press, 1905), p. 59.
4. *Hamlet*, III.ii.10–12, 21–4. *William Shakespeare: The Complete Works*, ed. Peter Alexander (London and Glasgow: Collins, 1951).
5. See, for example, Stephen Gosson's *The Schoole of Abuse* (1579) and *Playes Confuted in Five Actions* (1582).
6. *A Shakespeare Companion 1564–1964* (Harmondsworth: Penguin, 1964), p. 88.
7. J. E. Neale: *Queen Elizabeth I* (Harmondsworth: Penguin, 1960), pp. 377, 387.
8. *The Boke Named The Gouernour*, ed. H. H. S. Croft (New York: Burt Franklin, 1967), Vol. 1, pp. 4–5. (This gives a facsimile text; in Tillyard, the passage is modernized and silently abbreviated.)
9. *The Elizabethan World Picture* [1943] (Harmondsworth: Penguin, 1963), p. 21.
10. The Earl of Essex was a friend of the Earl of Southampton. Shakespeare's *Venus and Adonis* and *The Rape of Lucrece* bear flattering dedications to Southampton, while *Henry V* (V, Prologue, 29–34) offers cordial wishes for the success of Essex's Irish campaign. Southampton conspired with Essex

against the Queen; and after their abortive rebellion, Essex was executed, while Southampton's death-sentence was commuted to imprisonment for life.

11. Introduction to *Macbeth* (London: Methuen, 1964), p. lxxii.
12. Sonnet 29, line 7.
13. Greene: *Groats-Worth of Witte*, p. 45; Ben Jonson: *Discoveries* (Edinburgh University Press, 1966), p. 28.
14. Introduction to *Measure for Measure* (London: Methuen, 1965), p. xxxii.
15. Wilbraham, Wilson and D'Ewes are quoted in *James I by His Contemporaries*, ed. Robert Ashton (London: Hutchinson, 1969), pp. 62, 63–4, 64.
16. Lever: Introduction to *Measure for Measure*, p. xxxiv.
17. *Basilikon Doron* in *The Political Works of James I*, ed. C. H. McIlwain (New York: Russell & Russell, 1965), pp. 12, 27, 52.
18. *1 Henry IV*, III.ii.39–91; *Richard II*, I.iv.23–36, II.i.200–210; *Julius Caesar*, III.i.63–70. Angelo's reference to the man who swoons amid the crowd (*Measure for Measure*, II.iv.24–30) more closely evokes the description of Caesar's swoon among the 'rabblement' at the Forum (*Julius Caesar*, I.ii.238–52) than the account of King James's mere annoyance at the throng during his visit to the Exchange.
19. *James I by His Contemporaries*, pp. 65–6. John Nichols: *The Progresses, etc., of King James the First*, Vol. I (New York: Burt Franklin, n.d.), p. 89.
20. *Calendar of State Papers .....*, Vol. X, ed. H. F. Brown (London: H.M.S.O., 1900), p. 126.
21. *James I by His Contemporaries*, p. 184.
22. *William Shakespeare: The Complete Works*, ed. Peter Alexander, p. xxix.
23. Lawrence Stone: *The Family, Sex and Marriage in England* (London: Weidenfeld & Nicolson, 1977), pp. 31–3.
24. *Shakespeare Man and Artist*, Vol. II (London: Oxford University Press, 1964), pp. 613–14.
25. *Palladis Tamia* (New York: Garland, 1973), pp. 281–2.
26. Chaucer: *Troilus and Criseyde*, I, 400–420; Petrarch: sonnet 88 ('S'amor non è').
27. *Troilus and Cressida*, I.iii.85–124.
28. Theseus: *A Midsummer Night's Dream*, V.i.2–22. Prospero: *The Tempest*, V.i.50–51.
29. Cf. sonnet 69, lines 11–14.
30. *Some Versions of Pastoral* (Harmondsworth: Penguin, 1966), p. 86.
31. Dryden: *Essays of John Dryden*, Vol. I, ed. W. P. Ker (Oxford: Oxford University Press, 1926), p. 165. Johnson: *Johnson on Shakespeare*, ed. Walter Raleigh (London: Oxford University Press, 1908; rpt. 1957), p. 75. Coleridge: *Shakespearean Criticism*, Vol I, ed. T. M. Raysor (London: Dent, 1960), p. 102. Hazlitt: *Characters of Shakespear's Plays* [1817] (London: Dent, 1907), p. 247. Swinburne: *A Study of Shakespeare* [1879] (London: Heinemann, 1918), p. 194.
32. Harmondsworth: Penguin, 1946; rpt. 1965; p. 22.
33. *Shakspere and His Predecessors* (London: Murray, 1896; rpt. 1930), p. 345.

5.1 Notes

34. *Shakespeare's Imagery and What It Tells Us* [1935] (London: Cambridge University Press, 1965), pp. 289–90.

35. *The Jacobean Drama* [1936] (London: Methuen, 1958; rpt. 1961), p. 260.

36. Maurice Ashley cites and supports the view that 'If ever there was an act in which the nation was unanimous . . . . . , it was the welcome with which the accession of the new sovereign was greeted'. *England in the Seventeenth Century* (Harmondsworth: Penguin, 1958), p. 9.

37. 'The Oedipus Complex as an Explanation of Hamlet's Mystery' in *American Journal of Psychology* (January 1910); subsequently 'A Psycho-Analytic Study of Hamlet' in *Essays in Applied Psycho-Analysis* (1923), and *Hamlet and Oedipus* (1949).

   Freud himself asserted: 'it was not until the material of the tragedy had been traced back analytically to the Oedipus theme that the mystery of its effect was at last explained'. ('The Moses of Michelangelo' [1914] in *Collected Papers*, Vol. IV [London: Hogarth Press, 1956], p. 259.)

38. 'Hamlet' [1919] in *T. S. Eliot: Selected Prose*, ed. John Hayward (Harmondsworth: Penguin, 1953), p. 108.

39. 'Postscript' (from *The Use of Poetry and the Use of Criticism*, 1933) in *T. S. Eliot: Selected Prose*, p. 110.

40. Leavis's essay was re-published in *The Common Pursuit*, 1952.

41. *Shakespeare's Problem Comedies* [1931] (New York: Ungar, 1960), p. 4.

42. ibid., pp. 79–80.

43. In the Introduction to the Cambridge edition of the play (1922; rpt. 1950, p. xxx), Quiller-Couch said: 'Isabella . . . . . is something rancid in her chastity; and, on top of this, not by any means such a saint as she looks. To put it nakedly, she is all for saving her own soul, and she saves it by turning, of a sudden, into a bare procuress . . . . .' (Schlegel, Ruskin, H. N. Hudson and others had seen her as saintly.)

44. Lawrence, op. cit., p. 111.

45. *Shakespeare's Problem Plays* (London: Chatto & Windus, 1950; rpt. 1961), p. 2.

46. ibid., pp. 133, 134.

47. ibid., pp. 123–4.

48. *The Problem Plays of Shakespeare* (London: Routledge & Kegan Paul, 1963, rpt. 1965), p. 6.

49. ibid., p. 70.

50. ibid., pp. 96–106.

51. Introduction to *Measure for Measure*, p. xci.

52. ibid., p. xcvii.

53. '*Measure for Measure* and the Gospels' in *The Wheel of Fire* [1930] (London: Methuen, 1960).

54. '*Measure for Measure* and Christian Doctrine of the Atonement' in *Publications of the Modern Language Association* LXI (1946), p. 1047.

55. 'Comic Form in *Measure for Measure*' in *Shakespeare Survey* 8 (1955), pp. 14–27.

56. The text is that of the facsimile edition of the 1560 Geneva Bible (Madison, Milwaukee and London: University of Wisconsin Press, 1969). This differs in small details from the text as quoted by Nosworthy.

57. Introduction to *Measure for Measure* (Harmondsworth: Penguin, 1969; rpt. 1983), p. 26.

58. ibid., p. 32.

59. *Basilikon Doron* in *The Political Works of James I*, ed. C. H. McIlwain, p. 37 Cf. *Measure for Measure*, I.i.29–35, III. ii. 254–7.

60. ibid., p. 37. The Duke is 'A gentleman of all temperance' (III.ii.231).

61. ibid., pp. 37, 38, 52.

62. ibid., pp. 24, 23.

63. ibid., p. 27.

64. ibid., p. 40.

65. ibid., p. 34.

66. ibid., p. 20.

67. ibid., p. 20.

68. See Lever, Introduction to *Measure for Measure*, pp. xliv–xlv.

69. ibid., p. xlvii.

70. *Narrative and Dramatic Sources of Shakespeare*, ed. Geoffrey Bullough (London: Routledge & Kegan Paul, 1963), II, 429.

71. ibid., II, 441.

72. The analogy is pointed out by P. R. Horne: *The Tragedies of Giambattista Cinthio Giraldi* (London: Oxford University Press, 1962), p. 113.

73. Bullough: *Narrative and Dramatic Sources of Shakespeare*, II, 462.

74. ibid., p. 513.

75. ibid., p. 476.

76. ibid., p. 466.

77. ibid., p. 498.

78. ibid., p. 453 (1; II.iii).

79. ibid., pp. 415–16.

80. Schanzer: *The Problem Plays of Shakespeare*, pp. 110–11.

81. In Samuel Richardson's novel *Clarissa* (1747–8), the virtuous heroine, having been raped, slowly pines to death.

82. The first view is represented by Sir Arthur Quiller-Couch in his Introduction to the Cambridge text (1922); the second by W. W. Lawrence (*Shakespeare's Problem Comedies*) and R. W. Chambers (*Man's Unconquerable Mind*, 1937); and the third by Levin Schücking (*Character Problems in Shakespeare's Plays*, 1922).

83. 'Study of Thomas Hardy' in *Phoenix* [I] (London: Heinemann, 1936; rpt. 1961), p. 476.

84. The plotting bears numerous signs of rapid improvisation and inconsistent re-writing, particularly towards the dénouement. To take only a few instances from the list offered by J. W. Lever (in the Arden text's Introduction, pp. xxii–xxiii):

    [In Act IV, scene iii:] The Provost, though urged to return swiftly, does not come back. Isabella, provided with a token letter and a verbal message for Friar Peter, and dismissed by the Duke, stays on after Lucio's arrival, with no later exit marked for her in the stage directions or implied in the dialogue. Lucio enters at line 148 with an anomalous 'Good even', though it is understood (lines 45, 69, 111) to be morning. If we continue to scene v, we find the Duke meeting Friar Peter at an unspecified place, and informing him that 'The Provost knows our purpose and our plot'. Soon after, Varrius appears – a character who has not been prepared for and whose identity is likely to puzzle an audience.

85. *Shakespeare's Problem Comedies*, pp. 39–54, 94–102.
86. See Fripp: *Shakespeare Man and Artist*, Vol. II, p. 601. The deception allegedly occurred in 1574.
87. See Ernest Schanzer: 'The Marriage-Contracts in *Measure for Measure*' in *Shakespeare Survey* 13 (1960), p. 85.
88. ibid., p. 89.

Part 3

1. Lever: Introduction to *Measure for Measure*, p. xiii.
2. This and the subsequent quotations from the folio are from *The Norton Facsimile: The First Folio of Shakespeare* (New York: Norton, 1968).
3. See Richard David's Introduction to *Love's Labour's Lost* (London: Methuen, 1956; rpt. 1965), pp. xx–xxi.
4. See *A Dictionary of the Proverbs of England in the Sixteenth and Seventeenth Centuries* (Ann Arbor: University of Michigan Press, 1966), p. 452.
5. 'The Renaissance Background of *Measure for Measure*' in *Shakespeare Survey* 2 (1949), pp. 79–80.
6. 'Measure for Measure: Quid Pro Quo?' in *Shakespeare Studies* 4 (1968), pp. 232–3.
7. In addition, her view differs from that of Jesus (Matthew V: 28):
   But I say vnto you, that whosoeuer loketh on a woman to lust after her, hathe committed adulterie with her already in his heart.
8. V.iii.273–6, 277–9, 282–8. *William Shakespeare: The Complete Works*, ed. Peter Alexander.
9. Introduction to *Measure for Measure*, p. xv.
10. '*Measure for Measure* and Christian Doctrine of the Atonement' in *P.M.L.A.* LXI (1946), p. 1035.
11. Nuttall: 'Measure for Measure: Quid Pro Quo?', p. 243.
12. 'How Many Children Had Lady Macbeth?' [1933] in *Explorations* (Harmondsworth: Penguin, 1964), p. 31.
13. *Johnson on Shakespeare*, p. 28.
14. *Shakespeare's Imagery and What It Tells Us*, p. 289.
15. This ambiguity is thoroughly discussed by William Empson in Chapter 13 of *The Structure of Complex Words* (London: Chatto & Windus, 1951).
16. Sir Arthur Quiller-Couch: Introduction to the Cambridge edition, p. xxxvii.

E. M. W. Tillyard: *Shakespeare's Problem Plays*, p. 128. John Wain: *The Living World of Shakespeare* (London: Macmillan, 1964; rpt. 1978), p. 95.

17. *Studies in Classic American Literature* [1924] (London: Heinemann, 1965), p. 2.
18. *Encyclopaedia Britannica* (14th edition), XX, p. 446.
19. These and other productions are discussed in Ralph Berry's *Changing Styles in Shakespeare* (London: Allen & Unwin, 1981), pp. 38–40.
20. Letter in *The Times*, 13 October 1971, defending Peter Brook's *A Midsummer Night's Dream*; quoted in Ralph Berry's *On Directing Shakespeare* (London: Croom Helm, 1977), pp. 9–11.
21. *The Wheel of Fire* [1930] (London: Methuen, 1960), p. 96.
22. 'Measure for Measure: Quid Pro Quo?', pp. 231–51.
23. ibid., p. 242.
24. ibid., pp. 238–9. Nuttall quotes the translation of *The Prince* by Ricci and Vincent (London, 1935), pp. 31–2.
25. 'Comic Form in *Measure for Measure*', p. 15.
26. Coghill quotes Langland's *Piers Plowman*, C Text, Passus VIII, line 126. (Translation: 'O fortunate fault! O necessary sin of Adam!')
27. Ferdinand de Saussure: *Course in General Linguistics*, translated by Wade Baskin (London: Owen, 1960; revised edn. 1974), p. 117.
28. 'The Structural Study of Myth' in *Structural Anthropology* [I], translated by C. Jacobson and B. G. Schoepf (London: Allen Lane, 1968).
29. ibid., p. 215.
30. David Lodge: *Working with Structuralism* (London: Routledge & Kegan Paul, 1981), pp. 18–19, 32.
31. 'The Argument of Comedy' [1948] in *Shakespeare's Comedies*, ed. Laurence Lerner (Harmondsworth: Penguin, 1967), p. 322.
32. ibid., p. 315.
33. *Collected Papers* IV (London: Hogarth Press, 1956), p. 233.
34. Provost: IV.ii.28–9; Pompey: IV.iii.1–4.
35. *Poetry and Prose of William Blake*, ed. Geoffrey Keynes (London: Nonesuch, 1956), p. 183.
36. Pierre Macherey said: 'The concealed order of the work is thus less significant than its real *determinate* disorder (its disarray). The order which it professes is merely an imagined order, projected on to disorder, the fictive resolution of ideological conflicts ..... The disorder that permeates the work is related to the disorder of ideology .....' *A Theory of Literary Production*, translated by G. Wall (London: Routledge & Kegan Paul, 1978), p. 151.
37. Terry Eagleton: *Literary Theory* (London: Blackwell, 1983), p. 145.
38. *An Introduction to the English Novel*, Vol. 1 (London: Hutchinson, 1967), p. 96. Kettle emphasized, however, that 'the inadequacies of Jane Austen's social philosophy are overtopped by other, more positive vibrations' (p. 98).
39. 'Towards a Socialist Criticism: Reclaiming the Canon' in *LTP* (*Journal of Literature Teaching Politics*), no. 3 (1984), p. 7.
40. *Eros and Civilization* [1955] (London: Sphere Books, 1969), pp. 165–6.

41. 'Political Preface 1966' added to *Eros and Civilization*; p. 13.
42. See Bakhtin: *Rabelais and His World*, trans. Hélène Iswalsky (Cambridge, Mass.: M.I.T. Press, 1968).
43. *The History of Sexuality*, Vol. 1, translated by Robert Hurley (New York: Pantheon, 1968).
44. *Literature in Protestant England, 1560–1660* (London: Croom Helm, 1983), p. 70.
45. ibid., pp. 72, 73.
46. 'Transgression and Surveillance in *Measure for Measure*', to be published in *Political Shakespeare*, ed. J. Dollimore and A. Sinfield (Manchester: Manchester University Press, 1985). (I quote the typescript.)
47. S. S. Prawer: *Karl Marx and World Literature* (London: Oxford University Press, 1976), pp. 94, 98, 181, 386. *Marxists on Literature: An Anthology*, ed. David Craig (Harmondsworth: Penguin, 1975), pp. 270–71.
48. *Shakespeare and the Nature of Women* (London: Macmillan, 1975), p. 308.
49. 'Was Shakespeare a Chauvinist?' in *New York Review of Books* (11 June 1981), p. 20.
50. *Shakespeare's Division of Experience* (London: Cape, 1982), p. 196.
51. *Still Harping on Daughters* (Brighton: Harvester, 1983), pp. 191–2.

5.2   Bibliography

(*i*)   Texts

A popular single-volume edition of Shakespeare's works is Peter Alexander's *William Shakespeare: The Complete Works* (London and Glasgow: Collins, 1951). The standard scholarly text of *Measure for Measure* is the Arden edition by J. W. Lever (London: Methuen, 1965). Texts with briefer scholarly paraphernalia include the Signet paperback, edited by S. Nagarajan (New York: New American Library, 1964), which contains a useful selection of critical material; and the Penguin edition by J. M. Nosworthy (1969).

(*ii*)   Contextual Material

Geoffrey Bullough: *Narrative and Dramatic Sources of Shakespeare*, Vol. II (London: Routledge & Kegan Paul, 1963).
Sir Thomas Elyot: *The Boke Named The Gouernour*, ed. H. H. S. Croft (New York: Burt Franklin, 1967).

The Political Works of James I, ed. C. H. McIlwain (New York: Russell & Russell, 1965).

James I by His Contemporaries, ed. Robert Ashton (London: Hutchinson, 1969).

J. Dover Wilson: *Life in Shakespeare's England* (Harmondsworth: Penguin, 1944).

E. M. W. Tillyard: *The Elizabethan World Picture* (Harmondsworth: Penguin, 1963).

F. E. Halliday: *A Shakespeare Companion 1564–1964* (Harmondsworth: Penguin, 1964).

Alan Sinfield: *Literature in Protestant England, 1560–1660* (London: Croom Helm, 1983).

Jonathan Goldberg: *James I and the Politics of Literature* (Baltimore and London: Johns Hopkins University Press, 1983).

(iii) Criticism

Samuel Johnson: *Johnson on Shakespeare*, ed. Walter Raleigh (London: Oxford University Press, 1908, rpt. 1957).

William Hazlitt: *Characters of Shakespear's Plays* [1817] (London: Dent, 1906).

Walter Pater: *Appreciations* (London: Macmillan, 1889).

Sir Arthur Quiller-Couch: Introduction to *Measure for Measure* (Cambridge University Press, 1922).

G. Wilson Knight: *The Wheel of Fire* [1930] (London: Methuen, 1960).

W. W. Lawrence: *Shakespeare's Problem Comedies* [1931] (New York: Ungar, 1960).

D. A. Traversi: *An Approach to Shakespeare* [1938] (3rd edition, 2 vols.: London: Hollis & Carter, 1969).

Roy Battenhouse: '*Measure for Measure* and Christian Doctrine of the Atonement' in *Publications of the Modern Language Association* LXI (1946).

Clifford Leech: 'The "Meaning" of *Measure for Measure*' in *Shakespeare Survey* 3 (1950).

E. M. W. Tillyard: *Shakespeare's Problem Plays* (London: Chatto & Windus, 1950).

William Empson: *The Structure of Complex Words* (London: Chatto & Windus, 1951).

F. R. Leavis: *The Common Pursuit* (London: Chatto & Windus, 1952).

Mary Lascelles: *Shakespeare's 'Measure for Measure'* (London: Athlone Press, 1953).

Nevill Coghill: 'Comic Form in *Measure for Measure*' in *Shakespeare Survey* 8 (1955).

Ernest Schanzer: *The Problem Plays of Shakespeare* (London: Routledge & Kegan Paul, 1963).

D. L. Stevenson: *The Achievement of Shakespeare's 'Measure for Measure'* (Ithaca, N.Y.: Cornell University Press, 1968).

A. D. Nuttall: 'Measure for Measure: Quid Pro Quo?' in *Shakespeare Studies* 4 (1968).

C. K. Stead: *Shakespeare: 'Measure for Measure': A Casebook* (London: Macmillan, 1971).

Rosalind Miles: *The Problem of 'Measure for Measure'* (London: Vision Press, 1976).

Ralph Berry: *On Directing Shakespeare* (London: Croom Helm, 1977).

Darryl J. Gless: *'Measure for Measure', the Law, and the Convent* (Princeton and Guildford: Princeton University Press, 1979).

Lisa Jardine: *Still Harping on Daughters* (Brighton: Harvester, 1983).

Political Shakespeare, ed. Jonathan Dollimore and Alan Sinfield (Manchester: Manchester University Press, 1985).

MORE ABOUT PENGUINS, PELICANS
AND PUFFINS

For further information about books available from Penguins please write to Dept EP, Penguin Books Ltd, Harmondsworth, Middlesex UB7 0DA.

In the U.S.A.: For a complete list of books available from Penguins in the United States write to Dept DG, Penguin Books, 299 Murray Hill Parkway, East Rutherford, New Jersey 07073.

In Canada: For a complete list of books available from Penguins in Canada write to Penguin Books Canada Ltd, 2801 John Street, Markham, Ontario L3R 1B4.

In Australia: For a complete list of books available from Penguins in Australia write to the Marketing Department, Penguin Books Australia Ltd, P.O. Box 257, Ringwood, Victoria 3134.

In New Zealand: For a complete list of books available from Penguins in New Zealand write to the Marketing Department, Penguin Books (N.Z.) Ltd, Private Bag, Takapuna, Auckland 9.

In India: For a complete list of books available from Penguins in India write to Penguin Overseas Ltd, 706 Eros Apartments, 56 Nehru Place, New Delhi 110019.

THE PENGUIN ENGLISH DICTIONARY

The Penguin English Dictionary has been created specially for today's needs. It features:

* More entries than any other popularly priced dictionary
* Exceptionally clear and precise definitions
* For the first time in an equivalent dictionary, the internationally recognised IPA pronunciation system
* Emphasis on contemporary usage
* Extended coverage of both the spoken and the written word
* Scientific tables
* Technical words
* Informal and colloquial expressions
* Vocabulary most widely used *wherever* English is spoken
* Most commonly used abbreviations

It is twenty years since the publication of the last English dictionary by Penguin and the compilation of this entirely new *Penguin English Dictionary* is the result of a special collaboration between Longman, one of the world's leading dictionary publishers, and Penguin Books. The material is based entirely on the database of the acclaimed *Longman Dictionary of the English Language*.

1008 pages   051.139 3   □

PENGUIN REFERENCE BOOKS

☐ *The Penguin Map of the World*

Clear, colourful, crammed with information and fully up-to-date, this is a useful map to stick on your wall at home, at school or in the office.

☐ *The Penguin Map of Europe*

Covers all land eastwards to the Urals, southwards to North Africa and up to Syria, Iraq and Iran * Scale = 1:5,500,000 * 4-colour artwork * Features main roads, railways, oil and gas pipelines, plus extra information including national flags, currencies and populations.

☐ *The Penguin Map of the British Isles*

Including the Orkneys, the Shetlands, the Channel Islands and much of Normandy, this excellent map is ideal for planning routes and touring holidays, or as a study aid.

☐ *The Penguin Dictionary of Quotations*

A treasure-trove of over 12,000 new gems and old favourites, from Aesop and Matthew Arnold to Xenophon and Zola.

☐ *The Penguin Dictionary of Art and Artists*

Fifth Edition. 'A vast amount of information intelligently presented, carefully detailed, abreast of current thought and scholarship and easy to read' – *The Times Literary Supplement*

☐ *The Penguin Pocket Thesaurus*

A pocket-sized version of Roget's classic, and an essential companion for all commuters, crossword addicts, students, journalists and the stuck-for-words.

PENGUIN REFERENCE BOOKS

☐ *The Penguin Dictionary of Troublesome Words*

A witty, straightforward guide to the pitfalls and hotly disputed issues in standard written English, illustrated with examples and including a glossary of grammatical terms and an appendix on punctuation.

☐ *The Penguin Guide to the Law*

This acclaimed reference book is designed for everyday use, and forms the most comprehensive handbook ever published on the law as it affects the individual.

☐ *The Penguin Dictionary of Religions*

The rites, beliefs, gods and holy books of all the major religions throughout the world are covered in this book, which is illustrated with charts, maps and line drawings.

☐ *The Penguin Medical Encyclopedia*

Covers the body and mind in sickness and in health, including drugs, surgery, history, institutions, medical vocabulary and many other aspects. Second Edition. 'Highly commendable' – *Journal of the Institute of Health Education*

☐ *The Penguin Dictionary of Physical Geography*

This book discusses all the main terms used, in over 5,000 entries illustrated with diagrams and meticulously cross-referenced.

☐ *Roget's Thesaurus*

Specially adapted for Penguins, Sue Lloyd's acclaimed new version of Roget's original will help you find the right words for your purposes. 'As normal a part of an intelligent household's library as the Bible, Shakespeare or a dictionary' – *Daily Telegraph*

ENGLISH AND AMERICAN
LITERATURE IN PENGUINS

☐ *Emma* **Jane Austen**

'I am going to take a heroine whom no one but myself will much like,' declared Jane Austen of Emma, her most spirited and controversial heroine in a comedy of self-deceit and self-discovery.

☐ *Tender is the Night* **F. Scott Fitzgerald**

Fitzgerald worked on seventeen different versions of this novel, and its obsessions – idealism, beauty, dissipation, alcohol and insanity – were those that consumed his own marriage and his life.

☐ *The Life of Johnson* **James Boswell**

Full of gusto, imagination, conversation and wit, Boswell's immortal portrait of Johnson is as near a novel as a true biography can be, and still regarded by many as the finest 'life' ever written. This shortened version is based on the 1799 edition.

☐ *A House and its Head* **Ivy Compton-Burnett**

In a novel 'as trim and tidy as a hand-grenade' (as Pamela Hansford Johnson put it), Ivy Compton-Burnett penetrates the facade of a conventional, upper-class Victorian family to uncover a chasm of violent emotions – jealousy, pain, frustration and sexual passion.

☐ *The Trumpet Major* **Thomas Hardy**

Although a vein of unhappy unrequited love runs through this novel, Hardy also draws on his warmest sense of humour to portray Wessex village life at the time of the Napoleonic wars.

☐ *The Complete Poems of Hugh MacDiarmid*
☐ Volume One
☐ Volume Two

The definitive edition of work by the greatest Scottish poet since Robert Burns, edited by his son Michael Grieve, and W. R. Aitken.

ENGLISH AND AMERICAN LITERATURE IN PENGUINS

☐ *Main Street* **Sinclair Lewis**

The novel that added an immortal chapter to the literature of America's Mid-West, *Main Street* contains the comic essence of Main Streets everywhere.

☐ *The Compleat Angler* **Izaak Walton**

A celebration of the countryside, and the superiority of those in 1653, as now, who love *quietnesse, vertue* and, above all, *Angling*. 'No fish, however coarse, could wish for a doughtier champion than Izaak Walton' – Lord Home

☐ *The Portrait of a Lady* **Henry James**

'One of the two most brilliant novels in the language', according to F. R. Leavis, James's masterpiece tells the story of a young American heiress, prey to fortune-hunters but not without a will of her own.

☐ *Hangover Square* **Patrick Hamilton**

Part love story, part thriller, and set in the publands of London's Earls Court, this novel caught the conversational tone of a whole generation in the uneasy months before the Second World War.

☐ *The Rainbow* **D. H. Lawrence**

Written between *Sons and Lovers* and *Women in Love*, *The Rainbow* covers three generations of Brangwens, a yeoman family living on the borders of Nottinghamshire.

☐ *Vindication of the Rights of Woman*
Mary Wollstonecraft

Although Walpole once called her 'a hyena in petticoats', Mary Wollstonecraft's vision was such that modern feminists continue to go back and debate the arguments so powerfully set down here.

PLAYS IN PENGUINS

- ☐ Edward Albee *Who's Afraid of Virginia Woolf?*
- ☐ Alan Ayckbourn *The Norman Conquests*
- ☐ Bertolt Brecht *Parables for the Theatre (The Good Woman of Setzuan/The Caucasian Chalk Circle)*
- ☐ Anton Chekhov *Plays (The Cherry Orchard/The Three Sisters/Ivanov/The Seagull/Uncle Vania)*
- ☐ Henrik Ibsen *Hedda Gabler/Pillars of Society/The Wild Duck*
- ☐ Eugène Ionesco *Absurd Drama (The Rhinoceros/The Chair/The Lesson)*
- ☐ Ben Jonson *Three Comedies (Volpone/The Alchemist/Bartholomew Fair)*
- ☐ D. H. Lawrence *Three Plays (The Collier's Friday Night/The Daughter-in-Law/The Widowing of Mrs Holroyd)*
- ☐ Arthur Miller *Death of a Salesman*
- ☐ John Mortimer *A Voyage Round My Father/What Shall We Tell Caroline?/The Dock Brief*
- ☐ J. B. Priestley *Time and the Conways/I Have Been Here Before/The Inspector Calls/The Linden Tree*
- ☐ Peter Shaffer *Amadeus*
- ☐ Bernard Shaw *Plays Pleasant (Arms and the Man/Candida/The Man of Destiny/You Never Can Tell)*
- ☐ Sophocles *Three Theban Plays (Oedipus the King/Antigone/Oedipus at Colonus)*
- ☐ Arnold Wesker *The Wesker Trilogy (Chicken Soup with Barley/Roots/I'm Talking about Jerusalem)*
- ☐ Oscar Wilde *Plays (Lady Windermere's Fan/A Woman of No Importance/An Ideal Husband/The Importance of Being Earnest/Salomé)*
- ☐ Thornton Wilder *Our Town/The Skin of Our Teeth/The Matchmaker*
- ☐ Tennessee Williams *Sweet Bird of Youth/A Streetcar Named Desire/The Glass Menagerie*

PENGUIN BOOKS OF POETRY

CLASSICS IN TRANSLATION IN PENGUINS

☐ *Remembrance of Things Past* **Marcel Proust**
☐ Volume One: *Swann's Way, Within a Budding Grove*
☐ Volume Two: *The Guermantes Way, Cities of the Plain*
☐ Volume Three: *The Captive, The Fugitive, Time Regained*

Terence Kilmartin's acclaimed revised version of C. K. Scott Moncrieff's original translation, published in paperback for the first time.

☐ *The Canterbury Tales* **Geoffrey Chaucer**

'Every age is a Canterbury Pilgrimage . . . nor can a child be born who is not one of these characters of Chaucer' – William Blake

☐ *Gargantua & Pantagruel* **Rabelais**

The fantastic adventures of two giants through which Rabelais (1495–1553) caricatured his life and times in a masterpiece of exuberance and glorious exaggeration.

☐ *The Brothers Karamazov* **Fyodor Dostoevsky**

A detective story on many levels, profoundly involving the question of the existence of God, Dostoevsky's great drama of parricide and fraternal jealousy triumphantly fulfilled his aim: 'to find the man in man . . . [to] depict all the depths of the human soul.'

☐ *Fables of Aesop*

This translation recovers all the old magic of fables in which, too often, the fox steps forward as the cynical hero and a lamb is an ass to lie down with a lion.

☐ *The Three Theban Plays* **Sophocles**

A new translation, by Robert Fagles, of *Antigone, Oedipus the King* and *Oedipus at Colonus*, plays all based on the legend of the royal house of Thebes.